manifest WEALTH & ABUNDANCE as you read

Stop Thinking About Your Money Problems, Upgrade Your Mindset with the Power of THANK YOU, & Embrace the Process of Giving the Money, Not Just Receiving It!

RAVI TEWARI

ravinimbus@gmail.com

https://www.amazon.com/author/neera

https://neera.ck.page/76f50bfa9d

Thank You, Universe!

I breathe in and fill myself with all the wealth & abundance the Universe has available to me.

ACKNOWLEDGEMENT

Thank you, Universe, the source of all creation, for letting there be abundance and selfless love.

I thank the Almighty **SHIV-BABA** for making this book possible.

I am grateful to ***Baji (Lalit Mohan Tewari, my father)*** and ***my mother, Late Mrs. Geeta Tewari,*** who gave me birth on this planet and made me capable enough to lead the journey of writing books.

My ***mother-in-law cum mother, Mrs. Manju Himthani,*** always loves, cares, and gives blessings to me, so I achieve success in my life; I'm grateful for her.

My wife Neelam, just because you are Neelam, thank you.

Mitesh Khatri, Som Bathla, thank you for being my mentor cum coach and allowing me to think in the right direction.

Siddharth Rajsekar, Nithya Shanti, Ken Honda, Wahei Takeda, Brad Yates, Gary Craig, Hew Len, and Joe Vitale, thank you for the inspiration; you all allowed me to acquire the necessary knowledge to make this book possible.

I cannot thank you enough for ***my entire family and the beautiful people around me*** who inspired and motivated me at every step I sought help.

Thank you enough, ***Amazon and social media;*** you know why!

And last, thanks to the ***readers, my teachers, friends, and random strangers,*** for being a true asset. Your motivation, love, feedback, and honest reviews always energize me and bring the faithful Ravi out from inside. Thank you for giving me the life experience and invaluable support along the way.

WHY MUST YOU READ THIS BOOK?

- Ever wondered what the ***difference between money goals and wealth goals*** is?
- Are you living in ***a mindset of lack and limitation?***
- Do you feel you are ***not good enough to make more money?***
- Are you searching for ***the keys to success and money abundance*** in your life but failing to find that?

Then, your **search ends here** as this book is now in your hands!

- **Manifest wealth abundance through the power of thank you**

I have written this book as a way to **help you create wealth in every part of your life!** It hands over to you the keys to a life of success, fulfillment, wholeness, and plenty. **It teaches you how you can be open and receptive to all the good and abundance in the universe.** After reading and implementing the practical advice mentioned in this book on developing a sense of wealth and abundance in times of fear and insecurity, **you start experiencing wealth**

abundance in your life. ***It takes your thinking to the next level where you realize that money is not just a number or a piece of paper, but it is much more than that.*** You recognize the ***divine energy of money*** and learn how you can attract it in abundance just by practicing and knowing **the power of Thank You!**

- **Identify and eliminate limiting beliefs about money**

Most of us have a lot of ingrained beliefs around money that can be really limiting, and we often don't even realize it. This book is **a practical guide that guides you in identifying your limiting beliefs about money and eliminating them** using some of the most profound techniques. This book teaches you to **unpack the myths of money scarcity** and how to **embrace the process of giving money, not just receiving it.**

- **Understand that - MONEY LOVES YOU, AND IT CAN BUY HAPPINESS**

If you think - money can't buy happiness, it comes only to those who work hard, asking for money for your services is bad, money is the root of all the evils, there isn't enough money around, having money is selfish, money is hard to earn and easy to lose, etc..- then this book can change all your beliefs and make you realize that **money can smile, it changes when it is given with a particular emotion,** and the energy with which it imbues us impacts not only ourselves but others as well. Overall, it makes you realize that if you love and respect money, the money will be drawn towards you with the same love and affection. **Money loves you if you love money;** it is as simple as that!

- **Upgrade your mindset and level up your wealth frequency**

Many of us are ignorant that the **real cause of our financial problems is not the money but our own frequency.** This book teaches you how to **work on wealth frequency** instead of fixing your money problems. Throughout this book, you learn to treat money as a welcome guest, allowing it to come and go with love, respect, and without resentment.

- **Receive my blessings**

This is not just a book but ***my blessings and divine wishes*** that may help you look at your life differently and transform your relationship with money.

May abundance come to you in many forms, and the universe shower its gifts upon you!

If you want to **strengthen your bond with money** and **manifest WEALTH ABUNDANCE as you read**, **grab this book NOW and start reading!** After reading this book, I promise you will definitely say - ***"Wow, this book is wonderfully divine! I've never thought of money this wonderfully! I am sorry, money; Please forgive me; I thank you; I love you! Thank you, universe!"***

Contents

1

Introduction - Believe Me, Money Is Not That Bad

Go, my friend (money); come with your family. Arigato!

- Neelam Himthani

I had a strong positive feeling toward money during my early school days. I was always puzzled why some people are wealthy while others don't even get one-time food for their survival or shelter to live in!

- Why is so much imbalance there in this universe?
- If this is something that can be solved or understood, why are people failing to do so?
- Why every one of us doesn't have the same feelings about money?
- Why do some people think it is easy to earn, and others believe it doesn't come easily?

- Why do you think you can't grow rich, or why are you afraid of losing money?

- Why does someone hesitate to talk about one's financial condition?

And many such questions, but, unfortunately, I had no answers!

Over time, when I grew young, I got several opportunities to closely understand the ***money game.*** As I went deeper into the concept, I could find answers to most of my questions. During my webinars, open talks, and workshops, I talk about money, money-mindset, wealth-abundance, money-energy, and its deep connection with human beings. It gives me immense pleasure to satisfy my clients by providing them the results and values they are looking for. It's always the feeling of fulfillment when people truly understand how easy it is to make money, **our best friend.** The most immense happiness for me is when, after attending my webinar, people have a smile on their faces and enough confidence that they also deserve money. They feel content no matter how much money they earn; it's not about the number they see in their bank account but their feelings about money.

I long wanted to write a book on wealth and abundance. I wanted to tell people how easy it is to establish a bond between yourself and money. I also wanted to break various false beliefs people have about money, e.g., money is the devil, having the desire for money is bad, money is the root of all our problems, money creates dis-harmony between relationships, rich people are not good, how hard I try I always lose money, making money is a struggle, etc. I wanted to make people realize that money is not as bad as they think.

My special thanks to **Ken Honda & Wahei Takeda** (I'll talk more about them soon). Their teachings and lifestyle inspired me to write and influence people about the importance of money energy and its relationship with us. I finished Ken's ***Happy Millionaire Mentality Abundance Course***, and finally, the day came, and I decided to write down all my experiences, knowledge, learnings, and case studies. The result is right in front of you, in your hands! I am sure that if you understand and apply the teachings as you read this book, you will see success blossom in your life.

NOTE: Before opening the secret gates of money and talking about the *money game*, I would like to inform you again that this is not just a book to read for amusement only, but a tool to enhance your wealth frequency and attract wealth in abundance as you read. I will encourage you to do hands-on as you read to get more clarity and understand the concept. So, I request you to carry a diary or notebook whenever you read this book.

Go and get your notebook and pen before reading further.

Hope you are ready now. Open your notebook and write down the answers of below questions as per your current understanding:

- What is money for you?

- Do you think there are differences between money and wealth? If yes, what are those?

- Write down your feelings for money, e.g., hatred, loving, insecure, effortless, difficulty in earning, devil, divine, etc.

- Are you comfortable enough talking to your friends about your financial condition?

- Are you comfortable talking about your salary numbers with your family members?

- Do you jealous of someone who has more money than you?

- How do you feel when you don't want to pay, but there is no other option than to pay, e.g., unexpected tax, broker fees, rent, late fees, accumulated credit card bills, unexpected medical emergency, etc.

Keep your answers safe, as we'll use them to understand and change your perspectives (if required) about money as you read this book. My aim is to make money as your *happy and smiling friend* so that you live a comfortable life with it. After finishing this book, you must have developed an abundant mindset to attract as much money as you want. At the same time, you should be able to respect and honor the money (in-flow and out-flow both) you encounter during your entire day. Finally, you'll realize that it's all about your feelings about money, not the numbers you talk or think about.

THE *MONEY GAME*

You intend to win the game whenever you play a game, right? Who wants to lose the game? Nobody.

Also, you want to perform well in the game and become the man of the match, right? At least, these are the signs of a true sportsman like me.

I remember my school days when I was the captain of my cricket team and always played to win and scored more in all the matches. In one of the final matches, I scored 182 runs and was still not out till the end of our inning. That absolutely filled all of us with confidence and delightfulness. It almost ensured that we would win the match as it was the highest score ever against the opponent team. And, of course, as expected, we won that match and received the big shiny trophy.

So, what do you think about how we could win that match? Is it possible to win any game if you don't know its rules or how to play it well? Is it possible to perform well in the game if you don't know how to make the right strategies at the right time for the next step? Chances are you may win one or two games without knowing the rules and strategies, but certainly, it will not work for your future wins. This is what I call a *'fragile win.'*

The same is true for the *money game*. You may initially see money coming to you in abundance, but eventually, you realize that you don't have enough. If you don't know the rules, don't know how to treat your money well, or have no idea how to make strategies to **make your money feel comfortable with you,** you may not be able to consistently win it. So, what is this *money game* all about? Let's deep dive and understand this in detail.

Check your notebook and observe your answer to the question - **What is money for you?**

The answer could be different for different people. For a kid, money could mean just a few papers and coins or a means to buy cookies and candies. For young adults, it could mean a way to fulfill their desires. For investors, bankers, and business owners, it could mean a way to invest more and grow their business worldwide and earn name and fame. It could be a peace of mind for some, but for others, it could be the reason to destroy their relationships and peace of mind!

Most of us are brought up in such an environment where we keep hearing from our elders - *"money doesn't grow on trees and is therefore extremely difficult to acquire," "you will come to know how hard it is to earn money when you start earning,"* and *"money comes to those who work hard,"* etc. This is how exactly we have been defining money since our childhood. We've conditioned our minds and put a barrier between ourselves and the money by listening to our elders, neighbors, and family members. And this *unseen barrier* doesn't permit us to welcome and embrace money in our life.

In reality, money is way different than we know about it. In addition to the meanings described above or what you wrote in your notebook, it is defined as *energy*. You are energy, I'm energy, and everything around us is energy. We influence each other when we come in contact. We engage in a value exchange and transformation cycle when we earn or use money. Value has energy.

Sir Isaac Newton (*great physicist and mathematician*) explained that every action has an equal and opposite reaction. This is a simple yet profound law of energy. In frustration, anger, sadness, or despair, you radiate the same feelings outward and, in return, attract similar energy from the universe. It becomes essential for us to learn how this principle is applied to the *money game*.

Of course, money is energy and brings many emotions - more than you can imagine. All of us are influenced and impacted by these emotions.

Let's do a little exercise to understand it better. Write down your answers to the below questions in your notebook in YES or NO only:

- Have you ever felt powerless when you see there are no savings for the future?

- Did you feel irritated while talking about your financial conditions?

- Are you ashamed of showing your salary slip to your family or close ones?

- Do you feel jealous and resentful when you see others having more money than you?

If any of your answers to the above questions is YES, you are living with negative feelings toward money! The energy you are attracting is sorrow, resentment, sadness, and insecurities. As a result, you start believing more negative things about money. In such cases, people get so depressed that they start doubting themselves. They start thinking they are not good enough and there isn't much they can do about it.

Now, let's look at the other side of it. Don't you feel secure when you see enough bank balance? Are you not delighted when you win a lottery out of the blue? Don't you feel relaxed when, one fine day, your old friend returns the money he had borrowed from you years back? Now, check your answers. I believe, for most of you, the answers are YES. If feelings like love, happiness, satisfaction, or contentment are wrapped up in your money, you start receiving the same. And as you receive those beautiful emotions or feelings, you reciprocate the same outside. You start feeling *there is enough money in the universe, and you deserve to own all of that.*

DO YOU KNOW WHETHER YOUR MONEY IS SMILING OR CRYING?

The key point, for now, is to understand that - *there is so much money in the universe spreading love, happiness, and* contentment. *But so much is also spreading hatred, sadness, and fear.* This defines two kinds of money: **Smiling Money** and **Crying Money**.

Whenever you spend or receive money with positive emotions or energy, it becomes **Smiling Money.** Smiling Money is the money you give or receive out of love, care, and pure intentions. When others receive Smiling Money, they feel the love and care along with that money. And in return, they give you blessings filled with love and care, and eventually, your wallet receives back the Smiling Money. In life, money can often help others in a way that nothing else can. For example, when someone is going through a very tough time, like losing their job but having responsibilities for their family, "blessings and prayers," "good intentions," and "motivational speech" might console them, but money can show them a ray of hope and bring smile on their face. This is Smiling Money!

Conversely, when you spend or receive money with negative emotions or energy, it becomes **Crying Money.** Crying Money is the money you give out of anger, despair, frustration, sadness, and impure intentions. When people receive your Crying

Money, they feel those negative emotions you have wrapped up in that money. They become sad, unhappy, stressed, depressed, and sometimes violent. And eventually, your own wallet attracts the same negativity, and money keeps crying there.

This is what I call ***the money energy game. It doesn't matter how much you earn or have in your banks. The only thing that matters is the intention or energy with which you give or receive your money. It's all about Smiling Money and Crying Money.*** Now, go back and check your wallet - *whether your money is smiling or crying out there.* The best part is that only you can experience this on your own. No one else can do it on your behalf!

IS YOUR MONEY CONTROLLING YOUR CURRENT STATE OF MIND?

Apart from *the money energy game,* I would like to tell you about the second game of money; I call it ***the money number game.***

Most of us are worried about our bank balance. We feel insecure, ungrateful, and sad when we look at the numbers in our bank statements. We avoid paying bills when we see high numbers there. We know we have to face reality at some point, but still, we keep running away from it; WE DON'T WANT

TO FACE IT AT ANY COST! As a result, we spend much of our time worrying about those numbers and resenting money. This creates an unhealthy relationship with money. We avoid talking about money and feel ashamed of discussing our financial status with other family members. This increases our chances of attracting resentful, ungrateful, and joyless money in our lives. So, why does this happen?

The biggest mistake we make here is focusing on the number we see in our bank statements. And that number keeps bothering us. What if I say the money you think you have in your banks is not really there! Got scared? But yes, it's the truth. The money you deposit in the bank goes somewhere in the market; it's like traveling in the air. Nobody knows where but definitely somewhere. So physically, your money is no longer there. All that remains are those numbers you keep seeing in your bank statements or smartphones. You think you have a certain amount of money by seeing those numbers. What if it's all an illusion?

Let's make it a little scarier. Suppose you check your bank statement one day and find that the balance is ZERO! You did not spend it anywhere; it's just disappeared. You call the bank and ask about your money, but they say - *"sorry, sir, your bank balance is zero."* They ask about the transaction history, and you provide them all. But they again say - *"sorry, sir, we still don't have any proof, and you don't have any money in your account."*

How will you prove the amount you deposited, the interest you earned, and the salary you received? Everything seems lost in just one minute!

So always remain happy, satisfied, and contented with the money you have in your pocket. Never let the bank balance down your current state of mind. Never feel low, disheartened, or ashamed of your bank balance. Embrace the money you currently have, smell it, love it, kiss it and say thank you to it! It will do wonders in your life.

The moral of the above teachings is to develop the habit of expressing positivity towards your money. Always feel positive, happy, wealthy, grateful, joyful, and satisfied while spending money. Pay all your bills and debts in a happy mood. Donate money with pure and happy hearts. Help someone and feel thankful. Rejoice when you receive money, regardless of how small or big. Feel rich no matter how much you earn. Remember, it's not about the number; it's about the emotions and energy you attach to money.

This is all about *the money game*. It can make a great *money magician* who can make any amount of money just by moving his magic wand. Keep reading it and start doing the magic as you read! In the forthcoming chapters, you'll learn more aspects of money and how you can earn it in abundance.

EXERCISE TIME

It's time for some exercise now. Are you ready? It will make you calm, relaxed, and optimistic about your money. This exercise will help remove any negative energy associated with your money. Please follow the below steps:

1. Hold your wallet, purse, box, or anything with money in your hands.

2. Close your eyes and take a deep breath.

3. Rub your wallet gently and feel the money it has; feel the touch of your money.

4. Now say - **I AM SORRY, MONEY... PLEASE FORGIVE ME MONEY... THANK YOU, MONEY... I LOVE YOU, MONEY...**

5. Repeat step #4 two more times.

6. Pause for 10 seconds and experience the profoundness and positivity you just created around you.

7. Now say - **GO, MY FRIEND... COME WITH YOUR FAMILY... ARIGATO!**

8. Pause for 10 seconds and feel a big warm hug from Smiling Money.

9. Now say - **MAY I BE THE CHANNEL OF MONEY-BLESSINGS FOR SOMEONE TODAY!**

10. Gently open your eyes, kiss your money and say - **I LOVE YOU & I DESERVE YOU!**

Do share your experiences after doing this wonderful meditation for money. I am reachable at: ravinimbus@gmail.com

WEALTHY POINTS TO REMEMBER

❖ You are energy, I'm energy, and everything around us is energy. We influence each other when we come in contact. We engage in a value exchange and transformation cycle when we earn or use money. Value has energy.

❖ All of us are influenced and impacted by the emotions money carries.

❖ There is enough money in the universe, and you deserve to own all of that.

❖ There is so much money in the universe spreading love, happiness, and contentment. But so much is also spreading hatred, sadness, and fear. This defines two kinds of money: **Smiling Money** and **Crying Money**.

❖ Smiling Money is the money you give out of love, care, and pure intentions. Crying Money is the money you give out of anger, despair, frustration, sadness, and impure intentions.

❖ It doesn't matter how much you earn or have in your banks. The only thing that matters is the intention or energy with which you give or receive your money.

❖ Be thankful for all the money you have. Be grateful for all the opportunities you get to make more money. No matter how much or how little money you are currently making, an attitude of gratitude is essential if you want in abundance.

I'm grateful for your learnings from this chapter and wish you receive in abundance. Thank you, universe. Arigato!

2

Is Your Wealth Frequency Down?

Financial peace isn't the acquisition of stuff. It's learning to live on less than you make, so you can give money back and have money to invest. You can't win until you do this.

- Dave Ramsey

The Pearl - *Buy from your friends who need your little support.*

Would you like to be a part of someone's dream? Would you like to be a part of someone's success story? Would you like to help someone to make them happy and feel special?

If yes, why not start with someone you already know and who needs your support as well? If your friend owns a business or starts a new venture, support them by buying their products... not by asking for something for free. Remember, **they won't ask for your support; they might not**

even show that they need your help. But, still, you move ahead and raise your hands to support them. Believe me, they really need you!

Yesterday night, my wife, Neelam, messaged one of our students who has just started her handmade jewelry business and asked her to send pictures of all the jewelry she has so that we could buy some of them. Even though Neelam is not a jewelry lover, nor does she buy them frequently, she intended to support our student's new dream. We wanted to make her feel happy, special, and confident about herself. When she received our message, we were utterly overwhelmed by her reaction. After receiving our order, she was so happy that we could see the tears of joy in her eyes from a distance apart. We cannot explain the divine blessings and satisfaction we got after this! This is what I call the magic of Smiling Money.

I remember one famous quote from **Steve Jobs** - *"You want to know who your real friends are? Start your own business and ask for their support."*

When you buy something from your friends, even though you know you can get a better price somewhere else, you contribute to the success of someone you know personally. When you support their small business, you support their dreams and ambitions. It creates a positive aura around us and helps to attract abundance in life.

Congratulations on reading this chapter and taking a big step towards improving your wealth frequency! Welcome to the world of abundance!

3 PROMISES TO MAKE

Before we begin, I would like you to make the below 3 promises with yourself and note them down in your notepad for future reference. Believe me, these will change your wealth frequency completely:

Promise #1: I promise not to work on my money problems during my entire wealth & abundance journey. I will work on my wealth frequency.

This is important because as you focus on your money problems, you keep questioning yourself - *"Why am I not able to earn more?" "Why am I not able to save money?" "Why is money not working for me but working for others?"* etc.

I call all these *blackhole questions*, i.e., *never-ending questions*. The more you think about those, the more you fall into their traps. If the answers to those questions were so simple, you could have solved your money problems long back. But your money problems did not change because your wealth frequency did not change! Right? So, during our wealth & abundance journey, we will focus on upgrading our wealth frequency.

Promise #2: I promise to start my day with 10 random gratitude points after waking up every morning.

As soon as you get up in the morning, you need to immediately say "thank you" for any 10 random things that come to your mind. Thank you is a sign of respect and gratitude to the person, place, or anything in your surroundings that has helped you or given you something. It signifies that you have not taken their help for granted and acknowledge that they matter. No better word than thank you can show your appreciation and convey your gratitude.

Promise #3: I promise to develop the habit of chanting below four sentences whenever anything negative happens in my life or whenever I need to cleanse any negative energy from my surroundings:

1. I AM SORRY

2. PLEASE FORGIVE ME

3. THANK YOU

4. I LOVE YOU

These are the four profound statements of the **Ho'oponopono,** a *Hawaiian prayer* that can give you complete control over your life. These 4 powerful statements hold a lot of healing energy when enchanted with emotions and feelings. It helps you let go of all the negative feelings and brings peace of mind.

MONEY FREQUENCY VS. WEALTH FREQUENCY

It is essential to understand the difference between **money-making frequency** vs. **wealth frequency**. Most people in this world have money-making frequency; they don't have wealth frequency. So, what is the difference between these two?

If you are working for money, you continue to work for money almost till the end of your life. That means, as far as you are working for money, money will come to you. The day you stop working, money stops coming to you. In this case, making money is directly proportional to the amount of work you do every day to earn that. In short, it is the **money-making frequency** if you work for money.

Technically, if you are working for the money, who is the master here? Money! Right? But to attract wealth and abundance in our life, we should be the master.

Conversely, if money works for you without your active participation, that is the **wealth frequency.** It doesn't matter whether you are working or not; money keeps coming to you.

Imagine -

- You are sunbathing near *Bal Harbour Beach*, enjoying your day, and money is coming to your bank account without effort!
- You are sleeping at night, lost in your dreams, and money is credited to your account without doing anything extra!

This is the wealth frequency! Now, you are the master!

Many of us have made our lives so busy earning money that we can't even take leave or a break and spend time with our family. Think - *Is there any use of such money if you don't have time to spend that?* Have you ever wondered why you work *so hard every day from 10 AM to 5 PM? Why are you putting your heart and soul into your work?* At the end of the day, you want to achieve freedom, time, relief, happiness, satisfaction, time for your family, etc., right? What's the point if you can't have peace of mind while working hard and earning all the time? It doesn't matter whether you make $10,000/- per month, $100,000/- per month, or $10,000,000/- per month if you don't have time to enjoy that money. 90% of the people are stuck in this frequency; i.e., *I work for money, and money comes to me!* Are you also in the same category, i.e., having money frequency? Think about it!

MONEY GOALS VS. WEALTH GOALS

Do you have goals like making $10,000/- per month, $10,000,000/- per month, or even more? If yes, then you have the money goals, not wealth goals! This means that even when you achieve your desired number, who is the master? Money or you? Of course, money! Right?

Conversely, wealth goals are - *You choose* ***to live your minimum luxurious life by choice without diligent work for the rest of your life.***

Many people have only and only money goals; they don't have wealth goals. Money goals have the money frequency while the wealth goals have wealth frequency. To manifest wealth, peace, and happiness in abundance, you must have wealth goals vibrating at wealth frequency.

MAKING YOUR WEALTH GOALS

Who doesn't want to always live a luxurious life? We all want that, right? But, did you ever think about what a luxurious life means to you? What would that be if you got an opportunity to define 'your luxurious lifestyle' which you would like to spend every day?

Let's understand this in detail and find out how we can identify or make our wealth goals. For this, you need to take out your notebook and follow what I explain below.

Step #1: Note down the *minimum luxurious lifestyle* you want to live every month *by choice.* Here you should underline the word ***minimum***; it's **not the maximum!** You may be wondering why not the maximum? The answer lies here - *Can you define or confine 'maximum'? Is there any maximum in spending money?* No! Right? So, you must choose the *minimum luxurious lifestyle* considering all the aspects like your holidays, eating outside, shopping, hobbies, etc.

E.g., For my *minimum luxurious lifestyle* - I want to live in a 4-BHK flat; I don't want any loans; I want to drive Mercedes-Benz; I want to explore different countries every year; I want to eat in a five-star hotel at least once in a month without looking at the price of the items; when I go to a shopping mall, I should buy what I need without looking at the price tag; whenever I contribute, I should not feel like losing money; I want to gift my family and friends on their birthdays and festivals without thinking about the expenses.

Note: Do not add crazy things as part of your luxurious lifestyle, e.g., traveling by private jet every day, spending millions in gambling every day, dinner at 5-star hotels every night, etc. Will you be really living this kind of lifestyle every day? Will you be dining out in a 5-star hotel every single night? No! Right? Here I'm talking about the *'lifestyle' - that we can do every single day of our life.*

I hope, now, you must be getting an idea about how to choose your *minimum luxurious lifestyle*. Do you think this kind of lifestyle requires millions of millions of dollars? The good news is - **not really!**

Tip: It is good to involve your family members in this exercise as they are also part of your luxurious lifestyle.

Step #2: Calculate the monthly amount required (approximately) for your *minimum luxurious lifestyle*. When I calculated mine, it comes to around half a million dollars per month, not more than that! You see, it doesn't require millions of dollars for a *minimum luxurious lifestyle*. So, what comes as your monthly number? Note that down in your notebook. That number is your ***wealth frequency number*** or, simply, the ***wealth number***.

Step #3: Decide to save or make **double** your *wealth number*, which needs to become your *passive income*. E.g., in my case, my wealth number was half a million; that means I need to save or make 2*0.5 million = 1 million dollars per month. So, calculate *'your final wealth number'* that you need to save or make monthly.

Are you thinking about why I asked you to double your *wealth number*? Here is why - **The wealth number you calculate today, practically, it will take approx. 5-10 years to achieve that. As we know, the inflation rate causes an increase in the level of prices of goods and services every year, so our wealth number also needs to be increased by the same amount. Hence, we decided to double the wealth number to arrive at our final wealth number to be safer.**

It is critical to finish all the above 3 steps before proceeding because the goal must be clear first. Until you know your *final wealth number*, you won't be able to manifest it! Right? It's like saying to the universe, *"make me financially free,"* without knowing what that means to you in the first place!

After calculating your *final wealth number*, you must understand how to achieve that. One of my mentors always encourages me to have at least 10 **multiple sources of income (MSI)** to achieve my *final wealth number*. And here is the strategy that works the best. You should have:

1) **8 sources of passive income,** i.e., you don't need to work anymore to get money from these sources. It means - money will automatically come to you from these passive income sources.

2) **2 sources of active income,** i.e., you still work to get money from these sources. It means - if you work, then only money will come to you from these active income sources. Active sources of income are also required because they make you feel busy and active. They remind you that you've some purpose in your life, as there is no meaning in life without purpose.

UNDERSTANDING WEALTH GOAL AFFIRMATIONS

Now, as we are consciously working on our financial freedom, let's manifest our future where we've more than enough of what we need; we are financially free! Wealth frequency affirmations help us focus on this "more than enough." These affirmations set a vision for our financial freedom, and they work because they are based on the **Law of Attraction.**

Jack Canfield, *an American author, motivational speaker, and co-author of the best-selling book series "Chicken Soup for the Soul"* says - that the **Law of Attraction** allows for infinite possibilities, abundance, and joy. It knows no order of difficulty and can change your life in every way if you let it.

Our life is constantly being guided and influenced by the universe's various laws and forces, and the most powerful of all is the **Law of Attraction**. Like the law of gravity, it is always in effect, impacting your life more than you can imagine. Once you know this universal law and how to use it, you can easily change your life as you want! This is because - *You are in a constant state of creation. Every moment you are creating your reality. With every conscious or subconscious thought, you are creating your future. You start attracting what you start thinking and believing.*

When I talk about the **Law of Attraction** and its power to the people for the first time, they start having doubts about whether it really works. And if you are also in that category and are skeptical about its magic, don't worry; you are not alone! My answer to you is - *"In the Law of Attraction,* ***DON'T ASK HOW. IT DOESN'T USE THE LOGIC; IT USES THE MAGIC. EXPECT MIRACLES!"***

So, are you ready to create magic in your life? If yes, note down the below wealth affirmations in your notebook. **You need to repeat these affirmations at least 10 times every morning just after you wake up**:

3) **Affirmation for your short-term goal for your monthly income:** Thank you, universe. Today is the last day of this month, and I've already made _____0.3 million dollars (write your desired number here)_____ amount of money happily and easily, just like the previous month, the previous month, and the previous month.

4) **Affirmation for your *final wealth number*:** Thank you, universe. Today is ____8th June 2027 *(the date which is 5 years from now)*____. I've already started making _____1 million dollars *(write your final number here)*_____ monthly income using 8 passive and 2 active sources. I'm now financially free!

Practice these affirmations every day and experience the miracles in your life.

Remember - *The entire universe is conspiring to give you everything that you want.* - ***Abraham Hicks***

LEARN WHAT IS STOPPING YOU FROM ATTRACTING ABUNDANCE

The opportunities are unlimited, and the universe is ready to offer you also, but your own frequency is creating the blocks. As a result, you always find a scarcity of money in your life!

Your frequency and limiting beliefs about money stop you from achieving your final wealth number. These beliefs are formed from many things you've seen around you, like family members, friends, social media, etc. Sometimes, you may also have collected beliefs about money from your own experiences with it.

A few examples of limiting beliefs about money are:

1) Money can't buy happiness.
2) Money comes to those who work hard.
3) All the people who have succeeded in life were successful because they had money.

4) Asking for money for your services is not good.

5) Money is finite. There isn't enough money around.

6) I'm born to live poor and die in poverty. I'll never have enough money.

7) Earning too much money is evil, or wanting more money is greedy.

8) Money is the devil and the root of all evils.

9) The rich get richer, and the poor get poorer.

10) I'm not good enough and don't deserve a lot of money.

11) Having money is selfish.

12) Having more money means inviting more troubles in life.

13) Money is hard to earn and easy to lose.

14) Money never stays with me. It comes and goes frequently.

15) More money will make you lazy and lethargic.

What limiting beliefs do you have about money? Having limiting beliefs about money doesn't stop it from existing. It prevents you from being able to improve your financial freedom. If you realize that the above toxic beliefs are impacting you, it's time for the inner transformation.

But before working on your limiting beliefs about money, take a pause & identify them within yourself. Go, get your notebook, and list them all. Unless you have identified your limiting beliefs about money, you won't be able to overcome those. Even though you may think you are absolutely positive about money, you will still realize your several hidden money beliefs when you do this exercise. You will come to know that lots of money blocks are there. Believe me! That's why it is very critical to finish this exercise with full attention before moving forward.

WEALTHY POINTS TO REMEMBER

❖ I promise not to work on my money problems. I will work on my wealth frequency.

❖ I promise to start my day with 10 random gratitude points after waking up every morning.

❖ I promise to develop the habit of chanting these four powerful **Ho'oponopono** sentences whenever anything negative happens in my life, or I need to cleanse any negative energy from my surroundings - I AM SORRY, PLEASE FORGIVE ME, THANK YOU, I LOVE YOU.

❖ You vibrate at a **money-making frequency** if you are always working for money. Conversely, if money works for you without your active participation, that is the **wealth frequency** you are vibrating at.

❖ Find out what goals you are living your life with - **money goals** or **wealth goals**. If you have dreams like making a certain amount of money every month, these are money goals. But if you *choose to live your minimum luxurious life by choice without diligent work for the rest of your life*, you are living with your wealth goals.

❖ To attract wealth in abundance, you must vibrate at a wealth frequency. For this, first, you calculate your wealth frequency number required to live your minimum luxurious life by choice without diligent work for the rest of your life. Next, decide to save or make double your wealth frequency number, which needs to become your passive income.

❖ You should have at least 8 sources of passive income and 2 sources of active income to live a financially free life.

❖ While working with the universe, don't ask how. Expect miracles!

I'm grateful for your learnings from this chapter. I wish you eliminate all your limiting beliefs about money and live an abundant life forever! Thank you, universe. Arigato!

3

Upgrade Your Wealth Frequency

When you send an intention out to the universe, the universe acknowledges it to you by saying - ***Tathastu*** *(i.e., so it is). If you say, "I am not good enough, and money doesn't work for me," the universe says -* ***Tathastu*** *(i.e., so it is). And if you say, "I am the money magnet and attract money from all directions," the universe still says -* ***Tathastu*** *(i.e., so it is). So, pay attention to your intentions!*

- *Ravi Tewari*

The Pearl - *The feelings of fear and gratefulness cannot co-exist. If you are saving money, do it with a feeling of thankfulness.*

Are you saving your money for your future? If yes, that's great!

Are you saving your money because you are afraid of your future? If yes, that's not great!

I have seen many people save money because they are afraid of their future. They keep collecting money in their bank accounts because they think they might get into some medical problems, lose their job, or something wrong may happen to them or their family. They save their money out of anxiety.

As you go through this book, you will realize that money is energy that flows easily with feelings of love, freedom, joy, and satisfaction. When you wrap the feelings of anxiety and fear with money, you repel money and eventually attract more anxiety and fear in your life. By doing this, you create more blocks to the flow of money. You keep on saving and, at the same time, adding extra layers of fear and anxiety.

No matter how much you save with these feelings, you will have anxiety and fear revolving around your future money. Do you think saving money with these feelings is a healthy saving? No, absolutely not. This is very contagious because initially, it starts with the feeling of saving for one week, and when you save enough for that week, you worry about the next month and start saving for that. Once you have enough for the month, you are afraid of the next 6 months and the following year. When you save enough for the entire year, you start fearing losing all that! So, you see that it's a never-ending cycle that keeps you anxious and worried all the time.

Do you know why you are so worried or anxious about saving money? Believe me, it's not related to money at all! It's because your mind has been programmed to act that way. Since childhood, you keep hearing from your parents - *"You should learn to save in anticipation of any mishappening. You need to take care of your rainy days well in advance."*

You think you are worried about money, but in reality, you are worried about the uncertainty and your inability to handle the circumstances. You doubt your strength and capability to face adverse circumstances and then put all the blame on money.

So, what should you do? Shouldn't you save for your future? Of course, you should save!

You should save your money while imagining the various positive and exciting ways to spend it. Don't save it with negative, fearful, and anxious feelings. Imagine your bright future and your money being spent on your fun travel, five-star dining, better education for your children, charity, and much more meaningful, fulfilling, and fun ways.

So, do you feel the difference? You realize that money is always there to support you, and you are always taken care of. Instead of surrounding yourself with negative and fearful energy, you are now infusing your thoughts of money with hope, love, appreciation, joy, and fun. If you experience these positive feelings for money while saving for your future, there will be no space for any negative feelings or fear, neither inside nor outside. Always remember that the feelings of fear and gratefulness cannot co-exist. All your anxiety and fear will disappear if you feel grateful. When you are grateful to the money, the money will also be grateful to you.

Therefore, ***if you are saving money, do it with feelings of thankfulness!***

As you understand from the previous chapter, your limiting beliefs about money are really holding you back. It's time to take actions that will help you begin to live your life to the fullest and let go of anything holding you back. But remember the promise you had made earlier - ***You won't work on your money problems; You will work to upgrade your own frequency!***

So, are you ready to live a life with an abundance mindset and become the best version of yourself?

Congratulations in advance on embracing your best version!

FEW TIPS THAT WILL CHANGE YOUR LIFE

This complete book is all about manifesting wealth & abundance, and you will learn several tips and techniques to achieve that as you read, but below I am starting with a few of them so that you can start working on them at the earliest.

1) **Have an abundance mindset with money:** Don't crib or perceive scarcity of money around you. Don't think that money is a limiting resource and is available only for a few selected "lucky people." *Money is a constantly renewable resource with an infinite supply.* The universe has everything in abundance and waiting for you to receive that. **Don't think it's not for you** when you see money around you. Always have the abundance mindset and keep welcoming the money.

During my webinars, when I talk about money abundance, most of the participants don't agree initially with what I explain to them. Most of them are not even ready to accept that they deserve abundance! They are not even ready to believe that millions of dollars could be in their bank account!

This shows how small thinking and narrow mindset they are living with toward money.

If you also feel that there is nothing in abundance in your life, then look around and observe - the air, grass, trees, mountains, sky, cells in your body, hair on your head, wrinkles on your skin, sounds in the atmosphere, words in your vocabulary, birds, insects, animals, and many such infinite things you can't even imagine.

It is actually true that everything you've ever wanted is more abundant than you ever dreamed. That's true abundance. Can't you live your life that way? Money is energy and is in abundance in the universe. The way you attract happiness and joy, you can also attract the "money energy." Your bank account may not seem sufficient to you at the moment, but believe that it deserves abundant "money energy" and was meant to be as plentiful as the leaves in a tree.

2) **Understand that your past can not dictate your future:** Many people make the mistake of living in their past. They make one of the biggest mistakes by thinking that the life they are born into is the life they are destined for. Who told you this "universal truth" about your life? Are you sure that you are too weak to take steps in your life and climb the mountain?

Let me give you a few examples to ease your burden and inspire you:

Oprah Winfrey, *the richest African-American of the 20th century and the most influential woman in the world,* was born into poverty in rural Mississippi to a teenage single mother and later raised in an inner-city Milwaukee neighborhood. She experienced considerable hardship during her childhood, saying she was raped at age nine and became pregnant at 14; her son died in infancy.

Sylvester Stallone, *iconic actor in three-Oscar-winning (ten nominations) Rocky*, struggled a lot in his past before beginning his Hollywood career. He was so broke that he became homeless, sold his wife's jewelry, and even sold his dog for $25 as he had no money to feed him anymore. But he kept believing that he could do more than he could ever imagine, and his past life could not dictate his future. This belief took him from being dead broke and sleeping on a bus station to being worth billion dollars today!

Tom Cruise, an American actor and the winner of three Golden Globe Awards, grew up in near poverty. The family was dominated by his abusive father, whom Cruise has described as "a merchant of chaos." He was beaten up many times by his father.

Frederick Douglass, an African-American leader of the abolitionist movement, was born into slavery, violence, and separation from his parents.

Dhirubhai Ambani, *the first Indian Entrepreneur to feature his Company on the Forbes 500 list,* was born in a middle-class family. His father was a school teacher. Ambani moved to Yemen at the age of 16 and worked there as a gas-station attendant in an oil company.

No doubt, we all have our own stories, but the best story of all is that *your past can not dictate your future*. It's time for a mindset shift now!

3) **Practicing the 6-step technique:** Practice the below 6 steps logical technique to eliminate your limiting beliefs about money. This is great for those who tend more towards the logical than the metaphysical aspects of life:

Step #1: Be ready with the list of your limiting beliefs about money. As instructed in the previous chapter, ensure that your list of all limiting beliefs about money is complete and ready.

Step #2: Pick one limiting belief to work on at a time. Eventually, you must shoot all your limiting beliefs but let's start by choosing one. I suggest picking the easier one, one you know is definitely false, like, *"All the people who have* *succeeded in life were successful because they had money."*

Step #3: Ask yourself why you believe this. Reflect upon your life and write down the instances and experiences that reinforced this belief. For example, you may have seen successful people around you who were born with the golden spoon in their mouths; social media stories and posts showcasing their success and luxurious lifestyle; you may have seen people investing a lot of money and becoming successful; etc.

Step #4: Ask yourself - Is this 100% true? Gather shreds of evidence that suggest this belief is false. Search and find out various examples where this statement was false. Write down every instance that indicates this belief is untrue – in the world for others and for you.

Step #5: Eliminate the limiting belief with positive visualization. Chances are, these beliefs have become so impinged on your psychology that they have become well-established thought patterns, often triggered by a certain type of event. Your practice now is to, *whenever you catch yourself thinking this belief,* ***IMMEDIATELY*** *counteract it with a strong image of the opposite.* For example, if you believe that the only reason why you are unsuccessful is that you have no money, next time you think this, focus on all the people who rose to fame and fortune, who came from more difficult circumstances than you. Start thinking about **Oprah Winfrey, Sylvester Stallone, Tom Cruise, Frederick Douglass, or Dhirubhai Ambani,** who were the same as you are right now.

Step #6: Repeat. Now choose the next limiting belief from the list and repeat all the above 5 steps until you finish the entire list. Remember to work your way up to your list from the easiest to the most difficult limiting beliefs.

THE MAGICAL TECHNIQUE TO ELIMINATE NEGATIVE ENERGY

EFT is one of the most successful psychology self-help techniques ever developed. It works by helping you cleanse any negative energy blocking you from finding your motivation. Using EFT, you can overcome anxiety and fear and find your confidence. EFT can rapidly reduce the emotional impact of memories and incidents that trigger emotional distress. Over 100 clinical trials have shown that EFT is effective for anxiety, depression, fear, worry, etc. EFT is part of a group of therapies called ***energy psychology*** because they are believed to affect the body's electromagnetic energy fields.

EFT combines acupuncture and mind-body methods developed by **Gary Craig** and supported by decades of scientific studies. It is a method for *rapidly releasing unpleasant emotions and even physical discomforts*. It uses fingertip tapping on various acupuncture points. For that reason, EFT is often called *"the tapping technique."* You gently tap your fingertips on different acupressure points while adding words describing your negative emotion.

The below diagram demonstrates various tapping points:

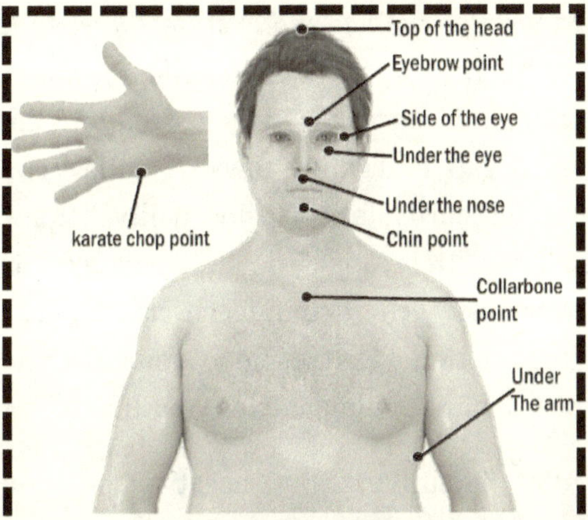

EFT Tapping Points

I encourage you to watch the standard procedure as explained by **Gary Craig** on YouTube. If you are reading this book on your mobile or laptop, you can simply CLICK HERE and watch that video.

I also encourage you to watch our EFT videos on YouTube. You can **CLICK HERE** and watch them.

EXERCISE TIME

Now, let's learn how we use this profound technique to eliminate our limiting beliefs about money.

First, recognize one of the negative beliefs or emotions toward money, i.e., what is the negative frequency about the money you want to release or cleanse? For example, *you may feel uncomfortable making huge money and even feel uneasy talking about making big money*; *you might feel jealous of seeing other person's money growth*. Similarly, other negative feelings toward money could be regret, insecurity, fear of losing, guilty, helplessness, meanness, stress, anger, doubt, anxiety, frustration, nervousness, lack of confidence, hatred, etc. These are the limiting negative energy you must release to attract wealth & abundance in your life.

After identifying the negative emotion, ask yourself this question (specific to money) - *On a level of 1 to 10, how intense is the feeling right now? 1 being very low, 10 being very high.*

For example, let's take one of my favorite examples I often use during my webinars -

- The **identified negative emotion** is - *feeling a lack of confidence in making money.*

- And the **level of lack of confidence** is *8,* which means a very high intensity of lack of confidence in making money.

Note: Here, *"a lack of confidence in making money"* is just an example. You should consider your negative emotion about money belief.

Now, we do one round of EFT and see how we feel about that emotion on a scale of 1 to 10 again. Kindly do it along with me by following the below steps:

Step #1: Repeat aloud three times the below statement while continuously tapping the **karate chop point** on either hand with two or more fingers:

"Even though I lack ***confidence in making money, I love and accept myself*** *exactly the way I am!"*

Step #2: Keep following through with step #3 and tap a few more tapping points. Remember to tap firmly, but not harshly, with the tips of our first two fingers, about seven times on each tapping point. The exact number is not essential; it can be a few more or less than seven. We can tap on either the right or left side of our body using our dominant or non-dominant hand. And, with every tap, we continue to repeat the *"reminder phrase."* The *"reminder phrase"* is just a very brief statement that reminds our system of what it is we are working on. So, in this case, our *"reminder phrase"* is the *"lack of confidence."*

Step #3: Here comes the first point. It is going to be the **top of the head.** Start tapping it about seven times with two fingers and say, *"this lack of confidence... release."*

Step #4: The second point is the **eyebrow point**, i.e., the beginning of the eyebrow. Start tapping it with two fingers and repeat, *"this lack of confidence... release."*

Step #5: The third point is the **side of the eye**, i.e., the outside edge of the eye socket. Start tapping it with two fingers and repeat, *"this lack of confidence... release."*

Step #6: The fourth point is **under the eye**, i.e., on the bony ridge of the eye socket under the pupil. Start tapping it with two fingers and repeat, *"this lack of confidence... release."*

Step #7: The fifth point is **under the nose**. Start tapping it with two fingers and repeat, *"this lack of confidence... release."*

Step #8: The sixth point is the **chin point**, i.e., between the lower lip and the chin. Start tapping it with two fingers and repeat, *"this lack of confidence... release."*

Step #9: The seventh point is the **collarbone point.** Start tapping it with two fingers and repeat, *"this lack of confidence... release."*

Step #10: The last point is **under the arms point**, i.e., about four inches below the armpit (for women, this is where a bra strap crosses). Start tapping it with four fingers, or just keep slapping gently and repeat, *"this lack of confidence... release."*

Step #11: So, that's simple enough! Isn't it? With that, we've now got the setup & sequence. After finishing the first round, let's assess & see how is the discomfort level now. How is our feeling of *lack of confidence in making money* now? What is the discomfort level now? Let's assume it is somewhat better now, and the discomfort level reduced to *4*. Well, OK, we went from *8* to *4*. It's about a 50% improvement. Yeah, that feels good. But we're not down to zero yet. So, we'll repeat the process from the **karate chop point** and re-assess once we complete tapping the last point. Well, maybe now we're two or zero, but we keep going until we reach zero discomfort level.

I hope you did this exercise with me and felt relaxed just after the first round. Imagine how you will if you do it continuously for 21 days to all your limiting beliefs about money! Believe me, they all will disappear!

I suggest you dedicate yourself at least once or twice a day, target one of the limiting beliefs, and practice 8-10 rounds of EFT to release that belief. It will work for you because it is based on scientific proof, not on concepts or knowledge from someone unknown! I am doing it personally and teaching it to hundreds of my students and clients; believe me, it does wonder every time!

Now is the time for **YOU** to do wonders by eliminating your limiting beliefs about money through this simple yet profound technique!

21 POWERFUL AFFIRMATIONS FOR WEALTH

Note down the below **21 abundant wealth affirmations** in your notebook. You need to practice these every day after waking up in the morning and before sleeping at night:

- ✓ I am open and receptive to all the good and abundance in the universe.

- ✓ I am always happy with money.
- ✓ I am the money magnet and happy millionaire. The prosperity of every kind is drawn to me.
- ✓ I attract money to me easily and effortlessly from all directions.
- ✓ I always have enough money than I need.
- ✓ Thank you, universe, for opening my new channels of wealth.
- ✓ I believe there is enough money for everyone. Thank you, universe.
- ✓ I love money because money loves me.
- ✓ I am open to receiving what is in the highest and best for all.
- ✓ I am open to giving what is in the highest and best for all.
- ✓ Today is a delightful day. Money comes to me in expected and unexpected ways.
- ✓ I release all resistance to attracting money.
- ✓ I am born rich and grateful for the money abundance I have.
- ✓ I attract money miracles into my life.

✓ I genuinely believe that we are here to bless and prosper each other. I reflect this belief in my daily interactions.

✓ I permit myself to feel wealthy and successful no matter how much I earn.

✓ I accept and receive unexpected money.

✓ I am appreciated and well-compensated wherever I work.

✓ I support others in becoming prosperous, and in turn, life supports me in wondrous ways.

✓ The money that comes to me today is a pleasure to handle. I save some and spend some.

✓ Money is a state of mind that supports me. I allow prosperity to enter my life higher than ever before.

WEALTHY POINTS TO REMEMBER

❖ The steps to eliminate your limiting beliefs about money are: **1)** Identify and list down all your negative beliefs about money. **2)** Promise to work on your frequency, not on the problems. **3)** Start developing the abundance mindset with money. **4)**

Understand that your past can not dictate your future. **5)** Pick one limiting belief to work on at a time. **6)** Ask yourself why you believe this. **7)** Ask yourself - is this 100% true? **8)** Eliminate the limiting belief with positive visualization.

❖ The **Emotional Freedom Technique (EFT)** is a beautiful way to flow and grow money. You can use EFT to create a balance with money. Tap out your old limiting beliefs about money, and then tap in the new beliefs to reframe and re-pattern your energy with money. The important tapping points are **1)** the karate chop point, **2)** the top of the head point, **3)** the eyebrow point (the beginning of the eyebrow), **4)** the side of the eye point (the outside edge of the eye socket), **5)** under the eye point (on the bony ridge of the eye socket under the pupil), **6)** under the nose point, **7)** the chin point, **8)** the collarbone point, and **9)** under the arms point.

I'm grateful for your learnings from this chapter. I wish you become an EFT master and eliminate all the negative money energy around you with fewer efforts. Arigato! Thank you, universe.

4

Beware Of Your Scarcity Mindset

Never surrender your hopes and dreams to the fateful limitations others have placed on their own lives. The vision of your true destiny does not reside within the blinkered outlook of the naysayers. Judge not by their words, but accept advice based on the evidence of actual results. Friends and family who suffer the lack of abundance, joy, love, fulfillment, and prosperity in their own lives really have no business imposing their self-limiting beliefs on your reality experience.

- Anthon St. Maarten

The Pearl - *Make someone feel loved, special, and appreciated.*

True happiness is not in receiving gifts we desire or the comforts we need; true happiness lies in how many gifts we give to make others happy. Your one act of kindness can make someone feel loved, special, or appreciated. It can make someone's day, bring smiles to sad faces or wipe tears from someone's eyes. It not only makes others feel acknowledged, but you also experience the happy and positive energy within - It's a win-win.

Nelson Mandela rightly said - ***"What counts in life is not the mere fact that we have lived. It is what difference we have made to the lives of others that will determine the significance of the life we lead."***

I have a few suggestions on how you can make someone feel special. I try these regularly; you can also try them. This is my secret (*now not anymore*) to attracting wealth and abundance in my own life.:

- **Write a message or email some random friends every week** and tell them how valuable they are in your life. Exclusively mention the qualities they have that you like the most.

- **Help your parents, partner, siblings, or family members** in cooking, dusting, cleaning vessels, cutting vegetables, or any house chores they do regularly, and never ask for help.

- **Surprise them with a gift.** It should not necessarily be something big or costly; it's mostly about your feelings and emotions wrapped up with the gift.

- **Hug them.** If distance permits, go and hug them. Your warm, close hug will tell them how much you love and care for them. Hugs will never go out of fashion, believe me. When you properly hug someone for an extended period - you share a moment of connection. You may even hug strangers (if this is something normal in your country and people don't feel offended), beggars, disabled people, or simply anyone.

- **Talk to them and listen to them.** Most often, older people want to say something or get heard. So, tell them that you're free to listen to them. It won't take much of your time but might bring a big smile to their faces. So, make this difference starting today.

- **Visit hospitals quite often** and serve the patients there without knowing their caste, creed, or color.

Congratulations on reading this chapter! I'm happy and hopeful for the new mindset you are developing as you read this book. Remember, it's not about how much you have or give; it depends on what emotions are wrapped up with money when you give. You have unlimited choices as opportunities are everywhere.

HOW WELL YOU CAN BREATHE IN AND BREATHE OUT MONEY

During most of my *wealth-mindset* workshops, I conduct one beautiful exercise that opens up the mind blocks of several participants they have about money. Would you like to do that exercise with me? If yes, here you go -

Close your eyes & take a deep breath in; take as much deep as you can. Now slowly and gently breathe out. Do it three times.

Take a pause and see how relaxed you feel by doing this exercise three times. You feel light, calm, controlled, and balanced when you are in this process of letting in and letting out.

Now, let's do this -

Close your eyes & take a deep breath in; take as much deep as you can. Now hold your breath, don't let it go out. If possible, close the nostrils of your nose with your fingers and make sure the air should not pass by. Keep holding your breath for as long as possible. After a few minutes, when you can't hold it anymore, try to breathe out **gently** and **slowly**.

Take a pause and observe how did you feel during this time? Were you light, calm, controlled, or balanced like before? Were you able to let out the air gently and slowly, or did you just let the air out as fast as you could? Did you feel relaxed during this entire process?

Here is one more for you -

Drink as much water as you can and eat as much food as you can. Now try to completely control your inner body system, mainly your bladder and intestine, and avoid going to the toilets for a few days. What do you think, can you do that? Of course, NOT! Our body is not meant to function this way. If you are letting something in, it must go out naturally. You can't hold something back for longer. If you try to go against this law, this will result in adverse consequences and may severely harm your internal system.

In fact, everything in nature works on the same principle. If you closely observe your surroundings, you will find that this law of *letting in* and *letting out* works wonderfully. Sometimes this becomes so profound and deep that we can't even realize or observe this happening. For example, nature *breathes the sunset in* and *breathes the sunrise out;* as a result, we enjoy beautiful evenings and vibrant mornings. It *breathes the Spring season in* and *the*

Winter season out, similarly to the rest of the seasons, and the weather cycle continues. How wonderful this is! Have you ever observed nature this way? Have you ever consciously observed tress's breath-in and breath-out process? Very rare, right?

And the final round is here -

Imagine the moment when you receive money for your work or the job you've done. You feel delighted, satisfied, secured, and joyful, right? Try to feel all the emotions and moments money brings to you. You embrace & welcome money as it comes to you, or you see it in your bank statement. It gives you a feeling of comfort and a moment to live without money resentment.

Now, recall the moments when you have to give money to someone else. For example, you pay your rent, phone bills, credit card bills, bank loans, or government tax. What emotions and feelings do you wrap with money before letting it out? Most people feel sad, crib, or resent money when it goes away with them. They begrudgingly pay their bills and are unhappy with money going far from them. They clink into the feelings of losing something. They want to hold and store money forever, and when it goes out, they feel disappointed.

Now, point to churn -

As we understand from previous chapters, we are energy, and money is also energy. We all are connected in one way or the other. Money flows in the universe exactly the same way as other energy particles do. The way we can't hold our breath for long, we need to breathe in/out continuously to remain alive; the same way, we can't have a permanent hold on money; we've to let it go. It also needs to follow the same *letting-in and letting-out law of nature.*

Money will come and go, as it must be in the flow. It wants to come to you but doesn't want to stay there forever. Its default nature is to follow *the breath-in* and *the breath-out* law. The sooner we understand this money law, the easier it becomes for us to feel free and positive about money, irrespective of whether it comes to or goes away from us.

CHECK - *ARE YOU WORRIED ABOUT MONEY SCARCITY?*

We live in a society where different people talk about money differently. There is no surprise if I say - most of us are negatively influenced by what we hear from our elders, neighbors, and family members about money. Since our childhood, the process of *"giving money"* has been wrongly portrayed in our subconscious minds as *"losing money."*

Most of us are worried about losing money because we think of money as a ***zero-sum game***, i.e., if someone else has it, we can't get it. We believe others are wealthy and have more; if they have everything, we can't get it. They have taken our share of happiness and money. I've heard kids saying that they cannot buy food from a good restaurant or cannot buy new clothes because their parents say *they are too poor to afford that.* Surprisingly, these innocent kids who can't even talk, stand, or walk properly know the meaning of *'being poor'* very well.

We've conditioned our minds to believe there is a limited amount of money in the universe and fewer money resources; if I give it to someone, I lose it forever. This thought of losing money scares us so profoundly that we start developing the scarcity mindset where we limit our ability to see the abundance in the universe. If we set the scarcity mindset, it becomes difficult to focus on anything else, no matter how hard we try. It is so subtle that we are often unaware of our scarcity mindset, but it exists inside. It requires a deep churning of our thoughts to find that out. Hence it becomes crucial to understand the scarcity mindset and how to deal with it better.

WHAT IS A SCARCITY MINDSET?

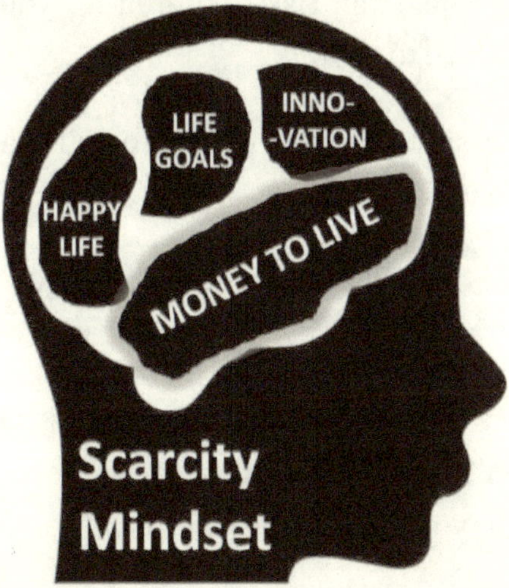

A scarcity mindset is when you are so obsessed with something you lack - mostly time or money - and you cannot focus on anything no matter how much effort you put in. It is a belief that money is limited, and one can run out or never have enough.

As you see in this picture, with a scarcity mindset, your mind is mainly filled with money-related thoughts. You continuously think about money problems and how to solve them.

Do you ever feel, think or do? -

- You're afraid to use your Emergency Fund in true emergencies.

- You're afraid of taking the financial risk, even the calculated risk, required for your business or work to grow.
- You stop yourself from dreaming and setting audacious goals.
- You don't invest because of the fear of paying extra taxes.
- You always feel you are lagging behind and don't have enough time or money to catch up with your colleagues or competitors.
- You don't show generosity to yourself or others even after being financially stable. You always crib about your money problems and not having enough.
- You think several times before using your credit cards.
- You keep thinking about your bank balance while enjoying good times with your family.
- The idea of going out for a vacation with your family and friends scares you so much.
- You have a habit of seeing your bank balance or investments regularly, even when those are not increasing.

- You quite often think - *I do not deserve to spend money on myself right now because I have to save for emergencies later.*

Above are a few examples of having a scarcity mindset. Of course, there are many, but I just wanted to give you an idea about them so you can identify your mindset about money.

A SCARCITY MINDSET STOPS YOU FROM GROWING

Scarcity mentality is the background noise your mind keeps making when it doesn't get enough of what it wants. Of course, it's not something you do on purpose, but it costs you.

In a 2017 experiment, researchers found that simply thinking about an expensive car repair bill significantly worsened the cognitive performance of low-income individuals. Here are some more consequences you face if you have a scarcity mindset:

- **Intelligent quotient (IQ) going down:** Based on research done on sugarcane farmers in India, who make most of their income at once - *At harvest time, they quickly grow from poor to relatively rich. The research shows that the farmers performed much worse on cognitive* *tests before the harvest when poor than after, despite controlling for stress and other factors. The researchers concluded that poverty "imposes a cognitive load and impedes cognitive capacity" and that these effects are equivalent to losing roughly 13 IQ points.* If you have an average IQ, losing 13 or 14 points can make it fall into the deficient category.

- **Limiting brain functions:** A scarcity mindset blocks your mind's doors and limits your outside-of-the-box thinking. It affects your ability to solve problems, gain information, and reason logically. Your brain becomes inefficient in making sudden decisions. Your mind continues to think about what you don't have, negatively impacting all other areas of your life, viz., health, relationships, career, and money. You become less productive at work or home. Chances are there, you may even make maladaptive financial decisions.

- **Feeling more stress and less confidence:** In a scarcity mindset state, your brain activity slows down in the **prefrontal cortex** (the area of the brain associated with decision making), much like a computer trying to process several user requests at once. The response time in decision-making becomes more extended, and as a result, you experience more stress and less confidence.

EXERCISE TIME

Now, it's your time to identify your own perception of money. Grab your notebook, be honest with yourself and write down all the thoughts that scare you about money. **List down every possible thought that stops you from giving money to someone else.** Take your time, don't be in a hurry, and think deeply to discover every single thought contributing to your scarcity mindset.

Wonderful! I believe now you'll have a long list of your *scarcity mindset symptoms*. You might be surprised looking at this list that you already have so many hidden reasons that may cause a scarcity mindset, and you were unaware of those till today! But don't worry. Now, when you know them, it becomes easy to learn how to deal with them.

THE ABUNDANCE MINDSET - *YOUR MAGIC WAND*

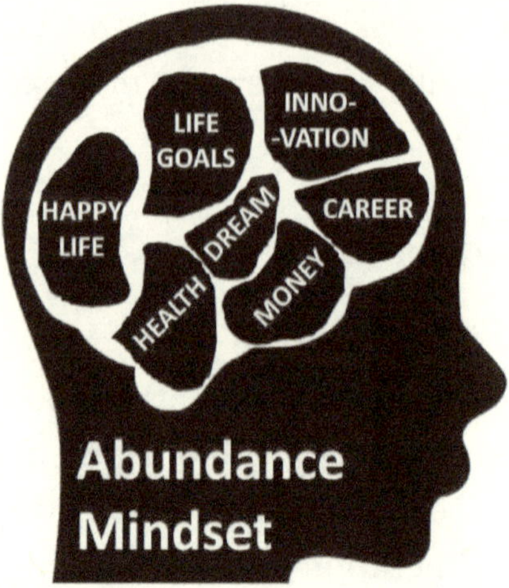

Before the scarcity mindset swallow you completely, let's learn to use the magic wand to vanish it forever. Believe me, making progress and having a better relationship with money is entirely possible.

First and foremost, you should **accept** that you deserve everything others are getting. As you see in the picture, you give equal priority to all areas of your life with an abundance mindset. You are no more focused on money problems alone.

But how is this possible? Let me explain to you.

We are living in an abundant world with enough money and resources for everyone. There is nothing in scarcity; the universe has everything in abundance. Let's open your arms and embrace the wealth & abundance the universe is ready to give you. And affirm loudly - ***Thank you, universe, for the wealth & abundance I receive. I welcome you into my life from all directions. I'm wealthy and financially free now.***

An abundance mindset is not only the belief that there is enough to go around but also expressing gratitude for what you already have. Having an abundance mindset means opening your mind up to money rather than living with your old limiting beliefs. You start living with an abundance mindset the day you start feeling enough in your life, you start seeing what you have around rather than only focusing on what is lagging, and you are no more afraid of losing money because you understand it will soon come back you. You start giving money in a joyful mood and opening the channels for sending and receiving more money & abundance. You'll feel that by giving money, you are serving others; you don't feel you are losing money and ultimately accept the *letting-in* and *letting-out* law of money. You effortlessly breathe in and breathe out money.

Stop feeling scarcity if some of your neighbors have won the lottery, don't feel jealous if some of your friends have bought a new car, don't feel sad if you did not get a promotion this year, don't feel down if your colleague got a salary hike but you did not, and don't feel sad while spending money or giving it to others. No one has taken your piece of the pie; if you think you also deserve to have it, soon, it is going to come back to you. It won't go anywhere. Look around, and you'll find many reasons to live an unlimited, complete, and satisfying life. If you are willing, you will find ways to be satisfied despite circumstances. You can easily develop the habit of giving and receiving affection and items of high value.

Let's not allow your limiting beliefs to stop you from living a life of abundance. The reality is not as complicated as what you have portrayed in your minds; it is far more accessible. As **Byron Katie** also says - *"Reality is always kinder than your thinking."* You just need to train your brain to sift through the thoughts, fears, and self-limiting beliefs to see a situation for what it really is.

During my money webinars, I meet various kinds of people and hear their different stories. Surprisingly, some of them are not even ready to accept that they can live a life of abundance! They are not willing to receive happiness and abundance in the first place. This shows how strongly they have conditioned their minds with their limiting beliefs.

If you are not ready to receive and take benefits, no matter how much money you have, you will never feel happy and satisfied. To attract wealth and abundance, you should be in a position to receive happily first. And receiving means - *being free to accept what is coming without any judgment; allowing yourself the freedom to receive.*

The abundance mindset is to enjoy and take full advantage of the opportunities coming your way. That is the time when you can create memorable and meaningful life experiences. Don't waste these magical moments just thinking about your *momentary adverse circumstances*. If you start praising for every act of your kindness, you will begin to feel secure and confident in your life endeavors and end up attracting more wealth & abundance.

This is the magic you can perform through this magical wand of an abundance mindset.

FROM A SCARCITY TO ABUNDANCE MINDSET

If you habitually think with a scarcity mindset, you tend to see one person's gain as your loss. Alternatively, an abundance mentality understands the limitless resources available to all of us. Never think that if more time, money, love, or attention is given to somebody, you will lose all that. In fact, it enriches your life, creating a sense of purpose through fulfillment and service.

Now, let's have some initial understanding of how we can break the ice and move towards an abundance mindset. This entire book I've written in such a format that at every step, you will be encouraged to move from your scarcity mindset to an abundance mindset. I have included various hands-on exercises that will make you feel confident and satisfied as you work on them.

1) **First thing first - Accept to receive:** Universe has everything in abundance; plenty is out there for everybody. You just need to be aware of that and have a mind and heart to acknowledge, receive and accept that.

The act of receiving is the most essential thing when shifting your mindset from scarcity to abundance. But I have often observed that people are not willing to accept the abundance of the universe in the first place itself. When money comes to them, they take it for granted and pretend as if they don't need it. When I pay someone a little extra for their services and appreciate their job, I often hear them saying - *"No, no sir, it's OK, I don't need extra money. This is part of my job, and I'm happy you liked my service, but I won't take extra from you."* They feel it will be unfair and not good if they get extra money for their services! We need to change this mentality.

Receiving means -

- Allowing yourself the freedom to acknowledge, receive and accept the positivity that is coming to you
- Knowing that you have inherent value that is worthy of receiving good things

Money wants to come and embrace you, but you are unwilling to accept it! Whose fault is this? If you aren't willing to accept happiness or abundance for the first time, how can it come to you the second time? Then, believe me, how much ever you earn or attain the status, you cannot be happy and feel abundant in your life.

So, as a first step, break this habit of limiting yourself from receiving what is coming to you. When you are doing a job or any kind of work, if you are paid extra with good and positive intention, accept that money. It is not the money you receive but the giver's blessings and positive energy. Acknowledge, receive and accept that.

2) **Be ready to give. Use your *Abundance Box*:** Unless you give, you can't receive. This is the most straightforward law of attracting wealth and abundance.

When I ask people how often they donate or give money to some needy, many of them answer the same: *"Not regularly. They give or donate money as and when they feel like to give."* And when I ask them why they are not regular in donating money, they say - *"They feel sad when their hard-earned money goes away from them. They feel as if they are losing something."* Many people resent donating money. They feel **'their money'** is going far from them.

This fear of losing money, holding it tight, and not giving it to some needy lowers your wealth frequency. Unless you break this chain of fear, you cannot be free to receive in abundance. ***The key to abundance is to give in abundance.***

If you want to feel free, joyful, happy, and contented while donating or giving your money, use your **'abundance box.'**

So, what is this **abundance box** all about?

The **abundance box** is the wealth box you use whenever you want to donate or give money to some needy. I personally have my abundance box and suggest everyone should have it. It is pretty simple to prepare your abundance box. Just grab any box with enough space to hold money and label it - ***"My Abundance Box."*** And whenever you receive any money, take a certain percentage amount from that (based on how much you can afford) and deposit it in your abundance box. *Make it a habit and promise you'll always deposit a certain amount of money in your abundance box whenever you receive any.* Soon you'll see your abundance box filling fast and growing rich. Now the money in your abundance box is not **'your money.'** It is for helping others and giving to needy people.

Next time whenever you need to give money to someone, take it out from your abundance box. Believe me, when you use your abundance box for helping others, you'll never feel as if you are losing **'your money.'** Instead, you will be filled with joy, satisfaction, and contentment.

Try it! I have been trying this for many years and experiencing miracles! Many people to whom I taught this method also started donating happily without realizing any money scarcity. They also started experiencing more blessings, best wishes, wealth, and abundance coming into their life. The more you give, the richer your abundance box becomes.

This is my abundance box:

EXERCISE TIME

Prepare your own 'Abundance Box' and use it whenever you need to donate or help needy people. *I love to see your beautiful abundance box if you share it with me at:* ravinimbus@gmail.com

3) **Count your gifts and blessings:** There is no particular time or moment when you think about how blessed you are. Think about all those moments, people, situations, or places that brought happiness or joy in your life. Even now, you will feel blessed when you recall those golden moments. Blessings and gifts cannot be measured by their weight or size; they are always powerful and can be received or given by anyone.

When you count your blessings and gifts, you note your life's beautiful things. You can feel special about yourself at any time. Counting your blessings is essential as it shows you many reasons you should express gratitude for everything you've received. It shows that you are grateful. Never take your gifts and blessings for granted. Always appreciate and be thankful for your good fortune and blessings before they are gone.

Now, let's take a few moments and write down all the gifts you have received so far in your life. I understand that the list may go long, but no worries, take your own time; you have enough pages in your notebook and ink in your pen. So, go ahead, and prepare a long list of your gifts and blessings.

4) **Check your pocket and focus on what you have:** The main problem with the scarcity mindset is that it makes you blind, and then you cannot see the real picture. You start interpreting on your own that - *"There are not enough opportunities outside," "I cannot get a new job as there are lots of competition," "I don't have enough skills to earn more,"* etc. You start seeing what your mind tries to show you.

Change this attitude. Stop being your own enemy. Instead of seeing the scarcity, check your pockets and see what you already have. Turn all your limiting beliefs around to thoughts like - *"There are enough opportunities, and I deserve it," "I've enough experience to get a new job," and "I am skillful enough as I've 12 years of experience in various IT companies,"* etc. And soon, you will witness the magic in your life in the form of a new job.

You've enough, but you ignore it and only focus on what you need next. And once you achieve what you need, you set your next target and become busy achieving that. And this never stops.

Believe me, as you start looking at what you have in your pocket, you will find that you have everything. You don't need to rush or go anywhere for happiness and money. You have enough of it. And soon, this new mindset will open the gates of more wealth and abundance in your life.

5) **Develop the habit of saying *Thank You*:** Practicing gratitude is one of the most profound and excellent methods to attract wealth and abundance in your life. *Express gratitude and feel happy for the overwhelming abundance you experience every day in your life.* **Oprah Winfrey**, *a famous American talk show host,* also says - ***"If you look at what you have in life, you will always have more. If you look at what you don't have in life, you will never have enough."***

When you look at **Wahei's** life journey (*I'll cover this in the next chapter*) also, you genuinely understand the power of ***Arigato (i.e., Thank You in Japanese).*** When you start expressing your gratitude, you realize how much you already have in abundance, and this awareness opens up the gate for more opportunities to come into your lives. **Tony Robbins**, *an American author, coach, speaker, and philanthropist*, also says, *"When you are grateful, fear disappears, and abundance appears."*

POWERFUL AFFIRMATIONS TO WIN OVER THE SCARCITY MINDSET

Here are some powerful affirmations that you can practice to develop the habit of gratitude in your life to attract wealth and abundance:

- ✓ Thank you, universe. I'm appreciated and well-compensated wherever I work.
- ✓ I am grateful to the universe for manifesting all the beautiful things in my life so far.
- ✓ With gratitude, I see the world in a new light. Each day is an opportunity and a gift. Money comes to me in an expected and unexpected way.

- ✓ Thank you, universe. Opportunities are everywhere. I've unlimited choices.
- ✓ I live in a loving, abundant, harmonious universe, and I'm grateful.
- ✓ I'm thankful that I'm now open to the unlimited prosperity that exists everywhere.
- ✓ I'm grateful for my life, and I trust it. It supplies all my needs in great abundance.
- ✓ Thank you, money, for supporting me in all possible ways. Now I allow prosperity to enter my life higher than ever before.
- ✓ Thank you, universe. Now I can move from a scarcity mindset to an abundance mindset, and my finances reflect this change.
- ✓ Thank you, universe. Now I pay my bills with love and rejoice as I write out each check. Abundance flows freely through me.
- ✓ I am grateful for my sense of gratitude - I know it is the way to joy, peace, and the life of my dreams.

You can learn and practice more on gratitude from **one of my best-selling books - Gratitude - Let the Universe Do Its magic.** I usually conduct the **"21 Days Gratitude Challenge"** every two months, covering various gratitude practices and exercises for the next 21 days. This brings many positive transformations to the participants, who discover a *"new person"* within them. If you want to join my community, you can reach me at: ravinimbus@gmail.com or click here.

WEALTHY POINTS TO REMEMBER

- True happiness is not in receiving gifts we desire or the comforts we need; true happiness lies in how many gifts we give to make others happy.

- A few secrets to making others feel happy are - write a message or email to some random friends every week; help your parents, partner, siblings, or family members; surprise them with a gift; hug them; talk to them and listen to them; visit hospitals quite often.

- ***Money will come and go, as it must be in the flow.*** It wants to come to you but doesn't want to stay there forever. It needs to follow the *letting-in* and *letting-out* law of nature. The sooner we understand this money law, the easier it becomes for us to feel free and positive about money, irrespective of whether it comes to or goes away from us.

❖ If you set the scarcity mindset, it becomes difficult to focus on anything else, no matter how hard you try.

❖ A scarcity mindset is when you are so obsessed with something you lack - mostly time or money - and you cannot focus on anything no matter how much effort you put in. Scarcity mentality is the background noise your mind keeps making when it doesn't get enough of what it wants. Of course, it's not something you do on purpose, but it costs you.

❖ An abundance mindset is not only the belief that there is enough to go around but also expressing gratitude for what you already have.

❖ The absolute truth is that there is nothing in scarcity; the universe has everything in abundance. Let's open your arms and embrace the wealth & abundance the universe is ready to give you.

❖ If you want to move from a scarcity mindset to an abundance mindset, first, you need to be ready to accept and receive what is coming to you. Then, prepare yourself to give using your abundance box. Always count the blessings and gifts you've received throughout your life. Focus on what you already have and be grateful for that.

I'm grateful for your learnings from this chapter and happy for your smooth transition from a scarcity mindset to an abundance mindset. Thank you, universe. Arigato!

5

Your Happy Millionaire Zone

I used to say why to save money if I die tomorrow, I haven't died yet, and I have nothing to survive on.

- Bangambiki Habyarimana

The Pearl - *Treat your money like your best friend.*

An interesting incident happened while I was writing this book, and I thought of sharing it with you.

Once, I and Neelam (my wife) went to ***MANOHAR***, *a famous restaurant in Bhopal,* and we often go there as we love to have coffee there. We parked our car outside and went inside to have some coffee. After spending some time, as we started to move from there, I saw a security guard standing near the exit door. He opened the door for us and gave us a beautiful smile. Neelam and I also smiled at him and thanked him for opening the door for us. That was when I also wanted to use *my smiling* *money*, so I took a couple of bucks out of my wallet and gave it to him. Initially, he was hesitant to take the money in front of many other people, but when I insisted, he took it with a timid gesture. I was so astonished by the behavior of that security guard that I thought of knowing more about his mentality about money. When I asked the guard why he was not accepting the money in the first place, he said, *"No, sir, I don't accept money this way. This is my job to open the door for all the guests either coming in or going out. I'm paid for that, so I cannot accept extra money from any guest."*

Does this happen to you also sometimes that you want to offer money with true, genuine, and happy feelings, but the receiver is unwilling to accept it? Is their behavior or mentality towards money good or bad? What do you say about it?

Many of you might be surprised by the answer, but such a mentality is NOT a happy relationship with money! If you reject the money coming to you, you stop prosperity from coming into your life. Many times, it's not about the money but the feelings of care and help wrapped with money.

I told the security guard - *"Never reject the smiling money coming into your life irrespective of how small or big it is. It's not the amount you receive; it's the positivity you attract. Treat money as your best friend. Always welcome it with a happy heart when it wants to come to you. Money also wants to be with you and needs your company. So, whenever money comes to you, feel like your best friend is visiting your house. Also, when money leaves you as you pay your bills, you should feel the same as if your best friend is leaving your house after having a good time with you. Bid the money goodbye with a cheerful and happy heart and say -* ***'It was really a nice time with you. Go safe and now benefit others. See you soon with your other friends!'"***

This is true that many of us treat money like a number that is only used to fulfill our needs. If the count decreases, we resent or feel sad; when it increases, we feel happy and secure. But, if we start understanding that money is not just a number but is wrapped with positive energy and various emotions, we'll start treating it as our best friend. We'll be happy and smiling whether we receive it or give it to others.

This is the real secret to attracting wealth and abundance in your life. The day you change your way of thinking about money, you open the doors of prosperity in your lives. Don't just have an "OK" relationship with your money; make it your best friend and feel grateful even when giving it to others.

Treat your money like any other meaningful relationship in your life. This relationship can provide you freedom, joy, security, and achievement in your life - just like any other beautiful relationship. Build trust with your money. Have faith that if it goes away from you, it will return too.

Our vision shifts when we consider that money comes along with love and various positive emotions. By broadening our scope of vision by a single degree, we gain access to a whole other reality - a reality that is much more aligned with our **Essence.** In fact, **money is a by-product of love, and it presents itself to us in the form of units of *Pure Love.*** Respecting, having fun, and loving your money will allow you to attract a wealthy and abundant life.

Whenever I personally give money to anyone, I always have this habit of saying - ***"Go, my friend, I had a beautiful time with you. You paid all my bills and provided me with all the comforts. Now it's time to go and bless others. See you soon with your other family members. Bye!"***

Congratulations on reading this chapter! I'm sure you are learning new things and developing an abundance mindset to receive and spread joy and happiness. I hope now you understand that being joyful, open to receiving, practicing gratitude, and feeling rich allow things and money to flow in and out effortlessly. I believe, after practicing these, you will add value to your own life and contribute something valuable to society as well.

WHAT YOU APPRECIATE APPRECIATES

What first impression comes to your mind when you hear the term **millionaire mindset**? What do you think what does the millionaire mindset mean to you? Does it mean earning or having millions of dollars in your bank account? Or is it about your net worth?

When I ask the same question during my wealth webinars and retreats, 90% of the participants relate it to their money or wealth. They directly or indirectly say that - a millionaire mindset is about making millions. But the millionaire mindset is not about how much you earn, spend or want to see in your bank statement. It's not even about your net worth, living in a luxurious apartment, or flying in your private jets.

A millionaire mindset is about living in abundance no matter how much you earn or have in your pocket. The idea is that millionaires live in a place of abundance that lets them experience tremendous success and confidence. Hence, even if you have less money but feel contented about that, can experience the abundance and enjoy every moment, are willing to help others financially, are open to receive opportunities as they come your way, and accomplish the goals you've always dreamed of achieving, you are already swearing by a millionaire mindset.

The key to having a millionaire mindset is to appreciate whatever comes your way. When you start appreciating something, it starts to appreciate you. Often people tell me that it's way more difficult to appreciate something troubling you for a long time. Sometimes people get so irritated with their situations that they don't even hesitate to commit crimes or do sinful actions. Such acts or mindsets can never solve your problem; instead, they could worsen your life. Once you learn to appreciate even your problems, you win over your hard times and setbacks. **Your problems are there to teach you some lessons; they have come to only YOU so that you can make yourself stronger and learn to answer life lessons. They have come into your life because the universe wants you to experience those challenges; learn how to come out of there; eventually, teach others**

how to face life challenges. How would you know to deal with your money problems if you never go through adverse circumstances? How would you inspire others from your life experiences if you have not gone through them yourself? How would you encourage others to handle life battles with ease and patience?

Problems are your temporary guests and will leave you once you stop entertaining them. Problems will always be there in your life; they will keep coming and try to trouble you, but if you understand ***the game of energy flow***, you can easily overcome all your challenges.

Problems and solutions are nothing but the flow of energy. When you look around, you see many things flowing from one direction to another. For example - the air is flowing, the water is flowing, and even your ideas are flowing in your mind. You go through the flow process when you talk to your friends, advise them, or even listen to them. There is a continuous flow of energy, money, or information.

With an abundance mindset, you feel happy about it when you receive money and then positively pass this happy energy to others. You receive money energy and let it go; receive it again and let it go again. This is the ***happy energy flow.*** The same is true for information. You learn something new, teach it to others and learn more...

Tony Robbins once said, **"Where your focus goes, energy flows."** This is true for any form of energy. It has to come and go and keep flowing in the universe. So, if you are going through any hard times or setbacks, remember the flow process and understand they will soon pass by. Start appreciating the process because what you appreciate appreciates. What you place your value on, what you choose to focus on expands or increases. It's essential to realize this because what you focus on DOES matter. It becomes the filter through which you experience life.

THE HAPPY MILLIONAIRE ZONE (HMZ)

You get into a happy millionaire zone when you start practicing an abundance mindset and believing that everything in this universe can be yours. ***It's not reserved for anyone; everyone deserves everything.*** If you want to change your perspective and limiting beliefs about money, you must remain in your happy millionaire zone. Being in this zone enables you to earn and give money in the same happy mood. You welcome money when it comes to you and when it leaves you, you say - ***"Go, my friend; come with your family. Arigato!"*** It doesn't differentiate whether money is coming to you or going out from you. Your inner state constantly vibrates at a higher frequency, and you remain stable and content with money. You become fully aligned with the happy energy flow.

When I talk to people, they define abundance in their own way. Someone relates it with having a luxurious lifestyle, while for others, it is about having extraordinary relationships. Someone may feel abundance when they are free to go anywhere they want; for some, it can be serving and contributing selflessly. And, of course, everyone has their own way of defining their financial freedom based on what values they want to live with. For me, I feel most abundant when I financially contribute wherever I want, whenever I want, without thinking about it. I feel more "wealthy" and happy when contributing to someone's life.

So, what is true abundance for you? According to you, what is your happy millionaire zone? Think deep and write that in your notebook.

The key to entering into your **HMZ** is - **Having an abundance mindset.** When in **HMZ**, you feel happy, safe, and secure as you live your day-to-day life. You are no longer affected by the money numbers, no matter how much you make or spend.

Once you trust in the flow of abundance, you start experiencing the prosperity that flows through you.

The HMZ is not only having material things or money to buy whatever you need but welcoming and accepting new things into your life is also a true nature of the millionaire mindset. As you start acknowledging and accepting things the way they are, true abundance flows through you. You become open to happily adopting any change in your life, and happy energy starts flowing through you. Any changes bring new positive energy into your life, create new flows, and as a result, you attract even more abundance and positivity in your life.

If you are unwilling to change yourself or accept the things they are, don't you feel your life will become static, and you will stop yourself from growing and learning? This is the point where you close the doors for wealth and abundance to enter your life.

The happy millionaire zone plays a vital role in your life as it provides you the mental ability and capacity to deal with different situations even when you feel overwhelmed. It shows you the path even during hard times or setbacks and gives you a sense of security and relief.

I've met with many such people who are doing great in their businesses and making enough money every month, but they still worry about - *what if they won't be able to earn the next month!* They live with a worry that something might happen and disrupt their stability. This increases their anxiety and distrust in the process of flow of abundance. But if they continue to be in their HMZ, trust the process, and believe the fact that - *"The universe is always there to take care of. It has never left you alone so far. You are blessed and will continue to live in abundance,"* it will give them a great sense of security.

Having money but living a life of worry and fear about money is never a happy millionaire lifestyle. You need to trust the flow of abundance. Trust in people; trust in your happy energy flow. Trust the universe that you will NOT be left alone. Remember - ***trust and abundance go hand in hand. Install this trust and belief in yourself that you are the beloved child of the universe and will be taken care of no matter what happens.***

EXERCISE TIME

- ✓ Make a list of your friends and relatives who would be there for you if life turned for the worst, emotionally and/or financially.

- ✓ The next time you receive money, write down all the positive emotions you feel at that moment. Also, think and write down all the blessings coming to you in the form of money.

- ✓ The next time you give money to someone or spend it, write down all the emotions you feel at that moment. Also, think and write down all the blessings you are wrapping up with the money before giving it to others. Feel that something positive is coming into your life as you spend or give your money.

As you start living in an HMZ, you start appreciating even when your money goes out. You develop a sense that money is there to serve everyone, not only humans but non-human beings as well. You start realizing that you are doing a service directly or indirectly when you give money. You start accepting money happily and spending it happily, too. This eventually increases the *happy money energy flow* in your life, and you begin attracting wealth and abundance.

IS THIS A MAGIC?

Most of the time, people wrongly take the idea of being in the happy millionaire zone. They sit idly and believe that the universe will shower blessing on them and make them wealthy and abundant. They think just keeping a positive attitude towards money will do all the magic without taking any action. But, remember that this is not how the magic of HMZ works.

Our actions are also energy. It will become stagnant if you don't allow it to flow in the usual manner. If you simply believe that everything will work out magically and don't take any action on your part to make it happen, it will be the same as not trusting in abundance. Trust means doing everything you can and then trusting that you will be okay because things will work out the intended way. It's not like hoping for the best without actually doing anything. Remember that no magic is going to happen unless you take any action.

I advise you to do your best with honesty and without any judgment, no matter what you are working on. This way, people will start trusting you and vice versa. This will always keep you in the happy millionaire zone, and you will automatically begin to attract wealth and abundance in your life.

Remember that your happy millionaire zone and positive energy flow are created based on how you approach your life. You are a happy millionaire if you accept, love, and embrace your life. Conversely, you are a sad millionaire if you reject, hate, or refuse your life. Now everything is in your hands; choose wisely!

WEALTHY POINTS TO REMEMBER

❖ Appreciate whatever comes your way. Because what you appreciate appreciates. It's not the amount you receive; it's the positivity you attract. Never reject the smiling money coming into your life, irrespective of how small or big it is.

❖ Don't just have an "OK" relationship with your money; make it your best friend and feel grateful even when giving it to others. Always welcome it with a happy heart when it wants to come to you. And bid him a goodbye when it leaves you.

❖ When money leaves you, develop the habit of saying - *"Go, my friend, I had a beautiful time with you. You paid all my bills and provided me with all the comforts. Now it's time to go and bless others. See you soon with your other family members. Bye!"*

❖ A millionaire mindset is about living in abundance no matter how much you earn or have in your pocket. Even if you have less money but feel contented about that, can experience the abundance and enjoy every moment, are willing to help others financially, are open to receive opportunities as they come your way, and accomplish the goals you've always dreamed of achieving, you are already swearing by a millionaire mindset.

❖ If you have an abundance mindset, you receive money with happy energy and pass it on to others positively. You receive money energy and let it go; receive it again and let it go again. This is the ***happy energy flow***.

❖ The key to entering into **Happy Millionaire Zone (HMZ)** is - **Having an abundance mindset**.

❖ The **HMZ** is not only having material things or money to buy whatever you need but welcoming and accepting new things into your life is also a true nature of the millionaire mindset.

❖ Remember - The universe is always there to take care of. It has never left you alone so far. You are blessed and will continue to live in abundance!

I'm grateful for your learnings from this chapter and wish you live in a happy millionaire zone forever. May you receive in abundance and spread in abundance. Thank you, universe. Arigato!

6

Wealth & Abundance Through The Power Of THANK YOU

Stop worrying about your money problems; upgrade your mindset and level up your wealth frequency. Use the power of THANK YOU for welcoming, accepting, and enjoying the process of giving money, not just receiving it.

- Ravi L Tewari

The Pearl - *Money can buy happiness!*

Probably you would have heard your elders saying - *"Don't run behind money; it can buy everything but not happiness."* We are so negatively influenced by this statement that we have firmly believed that money really can't buy happiness.

What is your opinion about this? Think profoundly and write it down in your notebook.

Now, take a moment and contemplate, does money really can't buy happiness, or are we assuming this belief just to comfort ourselves because we don't have enough money? Check, are we saying this just because of jealousy, as some of our neighbors have more money than us, and we can't afford the comforts they do? We need to be true to ourselves here and think - are we only consoling ourselves by saying that we don't need extra money for our happiness and trying to be happy with our little money?

If money can't buy happiness, why are we all running behind it and putting all our efforts and strength into earning more and more every single day? Why is there so much competition in the money area? Why are people ready to commit crimes to get more money? Why do we all need money so desperately if money can't give us happiness?

Do we all earn money and need more and more money to be UNHAPPY?

NO, right?

Imagine how your children feel when you buy them their favorite chocolates? When you give food or clothes to needy people, how do they react? What happens when you give a surprise gift to your wife or husband?

Now think deeply, what did you actually buy for them with money - a few tangible items or real happiness?

For them, having money is like having a magic wand using which they can reveal anything they want. Remember, money is all about exchanging emotions. You can't exchange happiness with others if you don't have money.

If you closely observe all the activities around you, you will find that your happiness is closely connected to money in one way or the other. For example -

- You are reading this book and feeling happy. Who made this possible? Money, right? Your money made it possible for you to buy this book.

- You are alive, enjoying time with your family, and having your favorite food daily; what made this possible? Money, right?

Here I have just given a few examples, but you can find hundreds of reasons why money is connected to every activity you do throughout the day and night.

Can you imagine a happy life without money?

Those who only understand the vague aspect of money and keep saying that money can not buy happiness must know that money is not only about a piece of paper or a metal coin, but it's way beyond what they can imagine. ***I feel sorry for money when I see people making it a target for all their wrongdoings. It's not the money that's the problem. We are the problem.*** We associate all our adverse circumstances with money and keep blaming money as the only reason for that. People with money scarcity experience emotions like anxiety, fear, shame, guilt, insecurity, or unsafe, leading them to avoid dealing with their problems and often worsen them. As a counter effect, such negative feelings reciprocate in a way that people start blaming their own situation of having less money rather than external environmental and societal factors.

There are so many emotions wrapped up in our money! It symbolizes a smiling or crying face and changes when given with a certain energy or emotion. If you give money in a happy mood, you radiate the happy energy; and if you are resenting while giving money to someone, you pass the sad emotions to the receiver and universe. Eventually, all these emotions bounce back to you and create your own circumstances. Happy emotions create a joyful environment, while painful emotions create a sad environment.

So, who is responsible for these circumstances? Money or WE?

Now think twice - ***Is it fair to buy all the happiness with the money you have and yet crib and say to money that - YOU CAN NOT BUY HAPPINESS!*** In my opinion, it's being disloyal and unfair with money.

Thank you for reaching till this chapter. You are here not by coincidence; it has some purpose, which may be hidden or not clear to you at this moment. But believe me, it's going to be a life-changing experience. As **Albert Einstein** rightly said - *coincidence is God's way of remaining anonymous.* So, trust your instincts and be ready to do the unexpected.

THANK FOR ATTRACTING WEALTH & ABUNDANCE

When life doesn't go the way you want, it's time to be thankful. Just say 'Thank You.'

Many of you must be thinking, *why*?

Here is the answer - Gratitude can attract blessings in the face of challenges. It is the healing energy for your bad health; it strengthens you when you are undergoing a broken relationship; it motivates you when you are struggling in your career, and it attracts wealth & abundance when facing financial challenges.

It gives you magical results when you start developing the habit of saying 'Thank You' many times during the day. You can just say it to someone, yourself, God, or the universe. ***One good thing about it is that it's not necessary you mean it every time you say it; it will gain meaning as you continue saying it and, without judging, proceed in your life.*** Soon you will realize its ripple effect as it continues to carry happiness, satisfaction, love, and joy from one person to another. And eventually, it returns back to you. You start attracting more opportunities, contentment, power, and abundance as a result of saying 'Thank You.'

GRATITUDE HELPS YOU GROW RICH

Gratitude is the energy that plants seed growing into unlimited wealth & abundance. It isn't just something that makes us feel good or contented; it also brings real-world prosperity and well-being to our lives. The gratitude energy upgrades all kinds of energy in our life, e.g., health, relationships, career, wealth & spirituality.

When you say 'Thank You' many times in a day, you start experiencing a different level of positive energy inside you. This high frequency helps you manifest wealth & abundance in your life. You start developing a different perspective altogether to see things and appreciate everything that comes your way as they are. You accept changes and learn from your mistakes. The *scarcity mindset* becomes an *abundance mindset*, and your *cribbing nature* transforms into a *grateful character*. Even during your hard times or setbacks, you are not shaken up. You remain calm and stable, which gives you more opportunities to think broadly and opens the doors to hope. Your positive and resilient attitude enables you to make the best of every situation that comes in your life. This helps you vibrate at the frequency of wealth & abundance.

Feeling grateful for the money you spend or payout carries love, joy, care & honesty and ensures you will receive more. I won't exaggerate if I say money has a magnetic thread connected to it. The same emotions return to you as you had attached to it before giving or spending. Positive emotions come to you if you attach care, help, love, and joy while spending your money. And if you attach grief, sadness, unwillingness, or fear before giving your money to someone, you attract negative emotions. The abundance you receive doesn't depend on the money you give but on how much grateful you are while giving.

Let me explain this to you by showing some experimental data.

Shawn Achor, *an American positive psychologist,* used **daily gratitude practices to help people change their thinking and behavior for the better.** His target audience included students, salespeople, CEOs, people from the US, Europe, Africa, etc. His research work showed the below excellent results:

- Productivity and sales increased by 37%
- Accuracy on tasks improved by 19%
- Chances of promotions increased by 40%

If you have the habit of being grateful and saying 'Thank You,' people love to connect with you and want to extend their business with you. Your grateful nature opens several opportunities for your career and helps you grow rich. Conversely, if you always complain and recent about your poor condition, people start avoiding you. Nobody wants to do business with someone with a scarcity mindset. I'm sure you also love working with someone who has a positive attitude, a smiling face, and a willingness to work without cribbing or complaining.

So why not be grateful and develop the habit of saying 'Thank You' if it can lead us to a wealthy and abundant lifestyle? Believe me, it's not that difficult; you just need to come out of your room and say 'Thank You' with a beautiful, loving smile to everyone you meet the whole day! That's it!

MY INSPIRATION - *A LIFE-CHANGING EXPERIENCE*

You may or may not have heard the name **Wahei Takeda**. I feel privileged introducing him to you through this book. When I first heard about him from one of my community mentors, **Ken Honda**, I was thrilled and thoroughly shaken up by the lifestyle, ideas, and philosophy he used to live with. ***Maro Up***, the best-selling book by **Ken Honda and Janet Bray Attwood**, is my core inspiration for writing this beautiful book. I'm genuinely grateful for that.

Here I would like you also to learn and understand **the power of 'Thank You'** Wahei Takeda believed all his life. This will enable you to be grateful for everything in your surroundings and eventually develop respect and love for money, not only what you receive but also what you give to others.

My blessings and best wishes to you - *If you practice and understand the power of 'Thank You' as described here, you will start developing the abundance mindset and attracting wealth & abundance in life. All this can happen as you read this book!*

WHAT INSPIRED ME ABOUT WAHEI TAKEDA?

Wahei Takeda was the *president and founder of Takeda Confectionery Co., Japan.* Often called **"the Warren Buffet of Japan,"** he was the most successful investor in the country, and no doubt he was the happiest one, too! He used to run one of the largest candy companies in the country, and the factory workers listened to children singing **'Arigato,'** which means **'Thank you,'** as they made this unique and trendy candy for babies. Wahei felt that the energy from the children singing while the factory workers made the candy was one of the reasons why his candy was a best seller.

According to Wahei, ***those in touch with 'maro' create a win-win situation for themselves and the people around them.***

What is ***maro***? The word is short for ***magokoro***, which means "a true heart - a heart with no deception or a façade," "sincerity," "To put your heart in a gift," or "Devote one's heart to something," in Japanese. It is the state of selflessness, the higher realm where humanity and the universe meet. ***Maro*** is the state where you start spreading selfless and unconditional love to everyone around you. It is the key to success.

Maro is very well connected to the feelings of Thank You.' The energy of 'Thank You' brings wealth & abundance to our lives. One psychologist's study proved that if people write a 'Thank You' note to someone on a regular basis, they experience a massive increase in their happiness scores. In fact, the good feeling lasts for an entire month. This can impact their financial life a lot. Wahei used this power of 'Thank You' to attract wealth and abundance throughout his life.

Wahei Takeda was born in 1933 in the port city of **Nagoya, Japan.** He was the son of a Japanese confectionery maker and the first of four children in his family. He learned all the secrets of making sweets and managing the family business in his childhood. As a young boy, Wahei saw that the people in his grandfather's village lived without depending on money, as people got what they needed through bartering during WWII. There he learned that **the roots of happiness lie not in money but in serving other people's needs**.

Wahei started realizing that if you have a pure heart and true sincerity, not only will people respect you, but the whole universe will start supporting you. He firmly believed in the power of **Thank You**. He understood that when we develop the habit of saying thank you, we start reading, writing, thinking, and speaking beautiful thoughts. As a result, we become beautiful, radiate divine love, and start attracting wonderful things in our life.

Though saying 'Thank You' is not directly associated with wealth, if we develop this habit, it also starts working in our financial favor, and as a by-product, we attract wealth in abundance. Wahei soon realized this fact and began his life journey with the attitude of gratitude.

At the age of 23, to make his career, he moved to **Hokkaido** and started his own confectionery factory. Unfortunately, it did not do well as per his expectation; in fact, it almost went bankrupt. But he did not lose hope.

During the '70s, Japan experienced a bowling craze. At that time, as many as 3,697 bowling alleys sprung up all over the land, and so high was the demand for the particular type of hardwood used to build the surface of the alleys that US suppliers warned that depleted forest stocks would take half a century to regrow. Seeing the vast opportunity in that field, Wahei also opened his own bowling alley, **"Waku Waku Ball."** But unluckily, the boom soon went down, and sales figures started declining drastically. This was another bankruptcy phase for Wahei. Again, he did not lose hope.

Do you think Wahei would have left the practice of paying gratitude after these mishappenings? No, not at all! He has always been able to deal with setbacks gracefully. He continued to be grateful for his adverse circumstances also. This was the main reason why his wealth frequency never came down. During his tough time, Wahei always showed courage and never lost patience. He always had the attitude to help others and believed that **setbacks open doors to opportunities.** He was far-sighted and always believed in making decisions considering all its future aspects.

When all his friends were also losing money and reaching bankruptcy due to the bowling era's downfall, he still had the attitude to help them in any possible way. When, one day, his friends came to him for asking help, he did not turn back; in fact, he took a loan from the bank to buy their bowling alleys.

His act of generosity paid him years later when the land prices again soared up.

If you can help people in need, they help you with their blessings. Many emotions like gratefulness, thankfulness, trust, care, love, etc., are wrapped in their prayers which fructify sometime in the near or far future. Wahei had also earned many such blessings throughout his life. By the time Wahei turned 40, he was living a financially free lifestyle with the belief that we manifest wealth in abundance if we show kindness, generosity, faith, respect, love, appreciation, and honesty towards money. He never had any negative thoughts about anything. He was grateful and contented with what he had and was always in the state of *maro*. He never had any uneasy feelings about any atom of the universe. He often said that - ***This universe is filled with divine energy, and we are all divinely created. By creating the thoughts of fear and insecurity, we manifest the same energy around us. If we only have the thoughts of love, trust, and care, there will be no fear around us.***

BUILT-IN TRUST

His philosophy about life and the level of thinking can easily blow anyone's mind up. The best example of this can be easily seen in his famous **Gold**

Museum. Despite being the most prominent VIP in Japan and spending most of his time in his Gold Museum, the property's perimeter was surrounded by mere bamboo trees. The fence was surprisingly low, the gate was wide open, and no security guards were appointed, which is relatively uncommon for a grand building like this. According to Wahei, the reason for this was - *"he wouldn't want to intimidate his neighbors, and besides, he didn't really need security guards because he had 'built-in trust.' And on the practical side, he wouldn't want someone sitting there all day long, doing nothing."*

How wonderful! His trust in people made him so down-to-earth and wealthy.

As opposed to that, we have developed so much fear within us about people and our surroundings that we are always worried about our money. We are always hiding our money from others. We believe that if others get to know about our money, we will lose all we have. As a result, we never open up to talk about our money. We keep saying - *I don't have enough, I don't earn much.*

Now answer this - *With this mindset, would you ever attract wealth and abundance in your life?*

The more you are worried about your money, the more gates you open for money to lose. So, what should you do?

The answer is here - ***You should stop feeling desperate or clinging to money. Allow your money to go with the flow. Develop the habit of saying 'Thank You.' This is the ultimate rule to manifest wealth and abundance in life.***

If you want to know the power of saying 'Thank You,' go ahead.

WEALTH & ABUNDANCE STARTS WITH THANK YOU

Throughout his life, Wahei practiced the habit of saying 'Thank You.' He knew the profoundness and the power of these two words. In Japan, they say **'Arigato,'** which means 'Thank You' in English. Wahei quite regularly practiced 'Arigato' in his life. He used to practice this technique hundreds of times a day and inspired many others to experience its power. He had so much faith in the power of 'Thank You' that he created his own product called *Arigato Baby Candy*. Even in his factory, workers listened to children singing 'Arigato' as they made this unique and trendy candy for babies.

Here is one of the beautiful examples from his life you will definitely appreciate.

Once, he met with a boy who was depressed, had lost all hopes in his life, was jobless, depressed, and unwilling to take action to win his life again. When Wahei listened to his depressing story, he wanted to do something for that boy and wanted him to realize the power of 'Thank You.' Wahei was a true believer in the magical power of 'Thank You' and wanted that boy to learn and accept that power too. So, he put a challenge in front of the boy and said - *"I would give you one million yen in exchange for one million 'Thank You's.'"* According to this deal, Wahei would pay the boy in monthly installments based on how many Thank You's the boy could say throughout the month.

The boy got astonished after knowing the deal and, at the same time, was not very optimistic about it but accepted the offer. And then he started saying 'Thank You' to everyone he met throughout the day. He did not care about the strangers or their reactions but continued saying, 'Thank You' to all because he wanted to receive as much money as possible from Wahei. He developed the habit of paying gratitude to the universe, God, and everything around him.

After one month, as per the deal, Wahei sent him hundreds of yens for his hundreds of Thank You.

The boy continued to receive money every month for every 'Thank You' he said. Slowly his condition started getting change. Soon after a few months, the boy's attitude changed entirely. The hopeless guy had now become a hopeful person; he had got a job now. He had attracted the girl of his dreams and brought his confidence back. Now he wanted to live a purposeful life.

When the young boy met Wahei again, he said - *"Now I've realized the power of Thank You. It has changed my life completely. I already knew the word Thank You but never realized that it could bring such magical changes in my life. It has the ability to attract abundance and positive opportunities in our lives."*

I hope you've gained some good insights after knowing the above incident. So, instead of worrying about money, my friend, start developing the habit of saying 'Thank You' to everyone you meet. When you get into this habit, you realize there are no limits to what you can and will achieve. You become worthy of the wealth you desire and attract more opportunities you can be grateful for. ***As you become the channel of blessings for someone, wealth and abundance begin to flow through you, and you open up to receive and give effortlessly.*** This wealth frequency releases all your money blocks and allows wealth to flow in. Eventually, it creates a positive impact on your life and the life of others too.

BE THE CHANNEL OF BLESSINGS FOR SOMEONE

You are lucky if you get the opportunity to become the channel of blessings for someone. Grab that opportunity and plant the seed of happiness into someone's life. Your one act of kindness will create a ripple effect in the universe, and everyone in the vicinity will be benefited.

Imagine a scenario -

One day you happily give some money to someone who is very hungry and needs food badly. After receiving the unexpected money from you, that person becomes so happy and joyful that he immediately rushes toward the nearby food court, gives that money to its owner, and buys some food. He gives you heart-filled blessings for the food he is eating because of you. After receiving the first order of the day after a long wait, the food court owner also becomes happy and delighted because now he can buy books and stationaries for his children. On the way to his home in the evening, he purchases the books and stationaries for his children. The children also become happy after receiving their father's surprise gifts. Everyone here is happy, and a chain of happiness has been created.

You see how the chain of happiness is created just by doing one act of kindness! Your first step became the starting link of the chain, and soon the entire chain was made. So, whenever you find an opportunity to become the link of a chain, grab it and start seeding the happiness!

May I be the channel of abundance blessing for someone today!

Wahei is a live example of this. He helped and served many people in his life without judging them. He believed in contributing with a positive mindset.

On one occasion, he bought a piece of land from some seller in **Nagoya**. The seller consciously overcharged him as compared to the market value. When Wahei's friends knew about the seller's cheating act, they asked Wahei to take some legal action against him. Wahei then did some little research and found that the seller was in serious debt, so he had to take that action. So, instead of feeling cheated or showing anger at him, he said - *"I am grateful that my money could be used in creating happiness for someone. I am happy because the seller is happy as he can pay his debt now and feel relaxed. I am happy because the* *person who received the payment is also happy. I am happy for everyone involved in this event."*

What a divine level of thinking!

AFRAID OF YOUR OWN FEAR, NOT MONEY!

There is an important aspect that prevents us from reaching our true potential, holding us back and not allowing us to live a life of wealth and abundance. That is FEAR. Fear of failure, not meeting expectations, or losing money - all these fearful thoughts lock us in the prison of comfort, and we don't want to come out of our comfort zone very easily.

Note that here I'm not talking about the usual fears in life, i.e., fear of death, fear of being physically harmed, etc. I am talking about the anxieties, the ego-threatening worries you face when you start working on your dreams and goals.

You might be surprised that 90% of your problems are related to the fear of losing something. We are afraid of losing money, job, or career opportunities because we are living a scarcity mindset. We think if we lose something today, we have lost them forever. We don't trust ourselves or our capabilities to earn them back again. We all are habitual in playing the **zero-sum game**, i.e., if someone else has something, we can't have it. We stop trusting people, the process, and everything around us. As a result, it strengthens our limiting beliefs, and unfortunately, we start attracting negative results and give birth to more fear. Fear is like a flu virus seeking opportunities to invade us. As soon as it finds someone vulnerable, it attacks them.

To get rid of this flu virus, we should start trusting people, giving them respect, honoring their opinions, and spreading love and harmony. We should begin to appreciate others and learn to feel contented in life. ***Let's stop feeling jealous if somebody is making more money than us; there is enough for us. Let's stop holding ourselves back by destroying the scarcity mindset; develop the abundance mindset by improving our relationships with ourselves and others; start appreciating our money; start trusting the universe that it has in abundance. I equally deserve it like many others.*** The virus can no longer live inside you if you have all these positive qualities.

The below inspirational incident from Wahei's life tells us how our inner fear becomes the reason for attracting the negative situations in our life:

Wahei always believed in kindness and helping others. His strong belief in the power of 'Thank You' had made him the wealthiest person in Japan. Despite being successful and rich, he had never appointed any security guard for his Gold Museum and residence. No proper alarm systems were installed to protect the exhibits in his Gold Museum. The reason was that he used to see the best in humankind and always treated people how he wanted to be treated; he had the trust, respect, and appreciation for people around him and no fear of losing money.

After the 9/11 tragedy, for the first time in his life, Wahei felt afraid. He was worried that his exhibits might get stolen or robbed, and keeping those in his museum might attract trouble for his staff and other members. So, he decided to keep everything securely in his house.

Ironically, the very next day, one intruder invaded his house and stole many of his valuable items, including various gold coins. Fortunately, the burglar could steal only a few dollars worth of items as most of the stolen gold pieces were replicas of the originals.

The following day when police came to inquire about the burglary, Wahei described all about the incident. Then, the police team promised to catch the burglar at the earliest. But, to everyone's surprise, Wahei told the police not to take any action against the intruder. It was not the intruder's mistake; it was Wahei's mistake. He further said - *"It was my feeling of fear that attracted the intruder and made him commit this mistake. Had he not been afraid and moved all the exhibits from the museum to his house, the intruder would not have taken this step. During my entire life, I never felt fear and had never attracted any such incident before. The day I attracted the flu of fear, I got the results in front of my eyes. I apologize and feel responsible for leading the intruder into committing this mistake."*

WEALTHY POINTS TO REMEMBER

❖ We must remove this limiting belief from our minds that money can't buy happiness. If you closely observe all the activities around you, you will find your happiness is closely connected to money in one way or the other. For example, your money made it possible for you to buy this book, read it, and feel happy. Can you imagine a happy life without money? NO, right?

❖ There are so many emotions wrapped up in our money! It symbolizes a smiling or crying face and changes when given with a certain energy or emotion.

❖ When life doesn't go the way you want, it's time to be thankful. Just say 'Thank You.'

❖ The power of 'Thank You' works as the healing energy for your bad health; it strengthens you when you are undergoing a broken relationship; it motivates you when you are struggling in your career, and it attracts wealth & abundance when facing financial challenges.

❖ The roots of happiness lie not in money but in serving other people's needs. If you have a pure heart and true sincerity, not only will people respect you, but the whole universe will start supporting you.

❖ Always have an attitude to help others. Believe that setbacks open doors to opportunities.

❖ By creating the thoughts of fear and insecurity, we manifest the same energy around us. If we only have the thoughts of love, trust, and care, there will be no fear around us.

❖ The power of "Thank You" has the ability to attract abundance and positive opportunities in our lives.

❖ May I be the channel of abundance blessing for someone today!

❖ Fear is like a flu virus seeking opportunities to invade us. As soon as it finds someone vulnerable, it attacks them. To get rid of this flu virus, we should start trusting people, giving them respect, honoring their opinions, and spreading love and harmony.

I'm grateful for your learnings from this chapter and wish you receive in abundance. May you develop the habit of appreciating everything that comes your way! Thank you, universe. Arigato!

7

Self-Esteem - A Key To Attract Abundance In Life

If we command our wealth, we shall be rich and free. If our wealth commands us, we are poor indeed.

- Edmund Burke

The Pearl - *I create my wealth and abundance from an infinite source, the universe.*

All material creation, everything you see, touch, hear, taste, and smell is made of energy and comes from the same source, i.e., the universe. You may refer to the source by various names like God, higher power, the holy spirit, etc. This source is, of course, beyond the perception of your five senses. The key to living an abundant life is accepting the idea that abundance comes from the universe. *If you are open to asking, ready to accept, willing to release any resistance from within, and relinquish negative beliefs about money, everything will be yours! The universe is ready to give all you deserve - more love, joy, wealth, and true abundance.*

True abundance begins with the thought followed by an intention - a clear understanding of what you want to have, or to happen, then an expectation, and finally, a strong feeling that lets you know that you deserve it. As long as you believe in this possibility, it serves you and others and brings harm to no one.

No matter how your past was, now is your time to enjoy all the fruits of abundance by connecting yourself directly to the universe and accepting what is waiting for you. Throughout the day, carry the sense of abundance with you reminding yourself of your true worth - **I create my wealth and abundance from an infinite source, the universe.**

Congratulations on reading this chapter! Practicing self-esteem is the key to eventually attracting wealth and abundance in our lives. This will bring values that are a *must-have* for the rest of our lives. Let's understand it in detail and start living with it.

A PROMISE TO WORK ON YOUR MONEY FREQUENCY

Before I begin this topic, I want you to make a promise that - *"Today onwards, you are not going to work on your **money problems**; You promise to work on your **money frequency.**"*

This will be one of the most crucial facts that most millionaires follow, and we also need to understand and implement it.

Have you ever met any millionaires and heard them saying - *"Money really doesn't bother me; I don't worry about it because I know I can earn more even if I lose it. My self-esteem and values are the most important things I care about."*

If you ask such millionaires if money really motivates them, what do you think will be their answer? They say - *"Money is not the only motivator!"*

Do you also want to reach this world-class millionaire level where you are not motivated by money but by your self-esteem and values? If yes, you'll have to start thinking like a millionaire, not how you have been thinking since childhood. Unfortunately, most of us are trying to become a millionaire because we are motivated by only money. We are focused on money numbers we want to make or earn daily. And believe me, this is not how the whole equation of wealth and abundance works. This is the *wrong path*. You cannot become a millionaire by letting money be your only motivator. You cannot attain wealth and abundance if you are only money-focused.

To learn this better, let me introduce two essential human aspects here: **MONEY-ESTEEM** & **SELF-ESTEEM**.

WHAT IS MONEY-ESTEEM?

According to the oxford dictionary:

- Esteem means - great respect and approval.
- Self-esteem means - a feeling of being happy with your own character and abilities.

The above two definitions lead us to define money-esteem as - ***a feeling of being happy with your money.***

Let me clarify about money-esteem in more detail.

90% of people in the world live with money-esteem and lack self-esteem. To understand this better, think about this question:

- When people make money, do their confidence and happiness level go up or down? And what happens the day they lose money?

If you reflect upon the above question, you'll realize that most of us feel encouraged when money comes to us and feel discouraged when money leaves us. If money comes, our happiness level increases, and if it goes away, our happiness level also drops. We've become totally motivated by money, and it has become our source of happiness.

If your sense of identity and self-dignity comes crashing down because of money, it's money-esteem. This is when you lose control of your happiness, and money starts taking that control. You start feeling happy or sad based on how much money you have in your bank accounts. You feel worthy and confident only if you've "enough" money. The moment money is gone, your self-importance is wholly gone.

If money fuels your happiness, confidence, existence, and worth, you are money-esteemed.

If money is taken away from you and you start feeling a lack of confidence or sad about it, you are money-esteemed.

I hope now you might be getting an idea about what being money-esteem means.

Now I would like you to reflect upon the below questions:

- How did you feel when you lost your money last time? Did you feel normal? Or did your happiness and confidence level go down?

- Did your satisfaction level go down or up the last time you had some loss in your business, lost your job, lost opportunities, or were cheated?

- Consider - you gave some money to one of your friends, and now he is not returning it to you when you badly need it. What is your reaction? How do you feel about it? Did your happiness level go up or down?

- Consider - you bought something expensive from a shopping mall, but immediately after buying it, you got to know that you could have got it at a lower price somewhere else. What is your very first reaction? Do you feel cheated? What is your confidence and happiness level now?

- Are you comfortable in a group where everyone except you makes millions every month? Do you feel weird or awkward in between them? Do you feel like - what to talk to them about, what to ask them, what to do there, etc.? Do you feel the odd man out? Do you experience the fear of missing out (**FOMO**)?

- Imagine - your spouse is not doing any work hence not making any money. How would you feel when you introduce him/her to your relatives, and they ask what he/she does? Be honest and think, what would you really feel about that? Do you feel guilty and ashamed? Would your happiness level go down, or would you remain unaffected?

If your answers to the above questions are mostly negative, think deeply - **Is this how a happy millionaire thinks, believes, or feels about money?**

No, certainly NOT!

So, why are you having such negative answers for money? What mistake are you making here preventing you from becoming a happy millionaire?

We are thinking and believing exactly the opposite of what millionaires think and believe, and then we are still hoping to attract wealth and abundance in our lives like them. We are living with wrong beliefs, which will never make our life wealthy and financially free as the way we desire.

If you carefully observe, most of us are living with money-esteem. We are comparing ourselves with people who make more money than us, and we feel guilty about it. We keep thinking that we are earning less and thrive on earning more. If you live with money-esteem, your money controls when and how much happiness and confidence you should have. Money switches your happiness button on and off. Money gets the remote control of your happiness.

This is definitely none of us want, right? We all want to live a life under our own conditions. It's a human tendency to live and act freely without being controlled by anything or anyone.

Believe it or not, the more desperate you will be to earn money, the less money you will attract in your life. **Your money worries attract more worries, making your life full of worries.** So, stop living with money-esteem if you want to be a happy millionaire. You should not allow money to control how happy and satisfied you need to be or how confident you need to be.

HOW TO MOVE FROM MONEY-ESTEEM TO SELF-ESTEEM

With the kind of money-esteem I discussed above, do you think you can attract wealth and abundance in your life? Do you think you can inspire your spouse to make happy money? No, absolutely NOT! Because money is controlling your happiness and confidence in every possible way.

If you want to move from your money-esteem nature to a self-esteem nature and attract wealth and abundance in your life, you need to learn to vibrate at a higher frequency. You need to master tackling money problems when they occur in your life. You need to learn to get into the right mindset when you see your money going away from you.

But the question is - **how do you learn that?**

For this, let's begin to sow the seed of abundance. Affirm this with me - ***"My happiness controls my money; My money doesn't control my happiness."***

You are precisely *living a life with self-esteem* when your money stops controlling your happiness. You gain control of your inner joy and satisfaction.

Briefly, self-esteem is:

- A feeling of security
- Feelings of competence
- How you see yourself (identity)
- A sense of belonging
- Self-confidence

Other terms often used interchangeably with self-esteem include self-worth, self-regard, and self-respect.

I define self-esteem as below:

I love and accept myself the way I am. Irrelevant of what I have or don't have in my life; irrelevant of who loves me or doesn't love me. I genuinely love and accept myself exactly the way I am with my current financial level.

I suggest you, going forward, do not work on your money-esteem. Start working on your self-esteem. Start loving yourself, and remain happy with yourself no matter how much money you have. And despite losing money, learn to be grateful, content, and confident enough that you can earn again. If somebody cheats you with money, have confidence that you can still make money. There is enough in the universe. You are living in an abundant world.

My favorite wealth affirmation is (you can also try) - ***Thank you, universe. I permit myself to feel rich no matter how much money I make.***

When transforming yourself from a money-esteem to a self-esteem mindset, it's vital to gauge whether you have started living with money-esteem or not. No matter what business or job you do or how smart you are, there will be profits and losses, ups and downs in your life. The richest man on this earth, no matter how smart he is, or the wealthiest woman on this earth, no matter how smart she is, will go through profits and losses in their lives. The important thing to note here is how you react to it. If you observe your reaction, you'll come to know whether you are living with self-esteem or money-esteem.

To check whether you are living with self-esteem or not, you can ask several self-esteem-based questions to yourself when you face any money problems in your life. Your positive answers to those questions will prove that you are living a life with high self-esteem.

For example, check the below sample:

Example #1:

Consider, you have done some shopping online, the product comes home, and unfortunately, it stops working just after 3 days. Further, the company is not willing to refund it as they've no refund policy. So, how do you feel about it? Does it change your happiness and satisfaction level? What is your first reaction to it? That moment decides whether you are living with money-esteem or self-esteem.

Let's refresh our promise:

I promise myself, from now onwards, I'll never allow money to control my happiness & confidence. From now on, my happiness will control how much money I deserve and make; my confidence will control how much money I have. Because I love and accept myself exactly the way I am, irrelevant of what I have or not, irrelevant of who loves me or not.

EXERCISE TIME

Take your notebook and write down the areas of your life where you promise to start practicing the idea of self-esteem, not money-esteem. These should prove that you are now working on self-esteem, not money-esteem.

For example:

- If I make a loss in my training or workshops, I still feel happy and satisfied.
- Even if someone is not paying my fees, I still have self-esteem and feel confident and satisfied.
- The day my sales are low in my showroom, I thank the universe and still feel contented.
- Even if I get rejected in my interview, I still feel motivated and satisfied.

- Even if I get fewer students in my school, I still feel happy, joyful, and satisfied.

All the above examples show our self-esteem. Similarly, you can write down the examples you would practice in your life daily.

If you have self-esteem in your life, your wealth and abundance frequency will automatically rise high. You start attracting happy money energy in your life and feel happy and contented even if the money goes away from you. Money starts coming to you; you don't need to rush behind; you don't need to be desperate about money. And if, for any reason, money doesn't come to you for a while, you will still be happy, confident, and satisfied.

WEALTHY POINTS TO REMEMBER

❖ If you are open to asking and ready to accept, the universe is willing to give all you deserve - more love, joy, wealth, and true abundance.

❖ I create my wealth and abundance from an infinite source - the universe.

❖ If your sense of identity and self-dignity comes crashing down because of money, it's money-esteem.

❖ Your money worries attract more worries, making your life full of worries. So, stop living with money-esteem if you want to be a happy millionaire.

❖ Self-esteem is - **I love and accept myself the way I am. Irrelevant of what I have or don't have in my life; irrelevant of who loves me or doesn't love me.**

I'm grateful for your learnings from this chapter and wish you transform yourself from money-esteem to self-esteem and start living a life of happy millionaires. Thank you, universe. Arigato!

8

Make Sure You Don't Play The Double Game

The mind is like water. When it's turbulent, it's difficult to see. When it's calm, everything becomes clear.

- Prasad Mahes

The Pearl - *The secret behind our so-called challenging relationship with money is our fear of losing it.*

Whether we accept it or not, most of us need money, and we love having lots of money, but we continue to have a challenging relationship with it. We continue to feel a scarcity of money or are unable to create a loving relationship with it. This happens because of the way we earn it or the way we welcome it in our lives. It's not only about earning but how we spend it is also unhealthy. If we are earning or spending money in unhealthy ways, how can we expect a good relationship with it? Whatever we are doing to make money - job, business, teaching, coaching, etc., if we are not happy with the process, i.e., the job itself, how can we expect a healthy end result?

The mistake most of us make is - We hate our jobs, are not willing to do it with joy or a happy mood, always do it with a cribbing attitude, don't do it with honesty, and do it just for the paycheck. All our stress and hatred towards our job sums up and are reflected back to us in the form of money. I won't exaggerate if I say that all our sufferings and negative feelings about our work are embedded in the act of getting money. So when we get our paycheck, we are hesitant to spend our hard-earned money. We recall the frustration, hard work, and stress we went through in the process of earning it, and, eventually, we end up fearing losing our money. We don't even realize that our negative attitude toward our job is causing this fear of losing money. As a result, whenever we think about money, a chain of feelings emerges from our minds, and we start feeling stressed, painful or irritated. Then we start cursing and blaming our money for not having enough and attracting these feelings of frustration.

If we closely examine the scenario, we'll find that all these feelings of frustration and fear of losing money originated from doing the job we dislike. If we are forcing and pushing ourselves hard to do the job we don't like, it's obvious that we won't allow the money to go without a damn good reason. We try to make all the possible efforts to keep our money with us and not waste it for any simple reason. In fact, we feel irritated or become sad when we see our hard-earned money going away from us. *If it's becoming hard to earn money, it becomes harder to let it go.* Also, this idea has been put into our minds by our parents since childhood - *We should not waste our money.* We have programmed our minds that *if money is going away from us, that means we are wasting it.* These memories suddenly pop up in the form of fear and stop us from spending more than necessary. And if we had to pay for something, we resent that.

These feelings of fear keep us busy thinking about *how much money is left over, how much more to earn, how much to save, etc.* These feelings are really not good for us. They can harm us in many ways, and sometimes situations can turn so bad that people don't even think twice before hurting themselves or committing any sinful actions.

So, if the relationship with money is so fearful, what about the happy, prosperous people around us? Do you know any person who is happy and prosperous? Can you please name that person?

So, what do all happy and prosperous people think about money? What do they feel or think while doing their business or work? What kind of relationship do they have with their money?

You will be amazed by knowing that they have totally different thinking and attitudes toward money in every aspect. They do the work they love and love what they do. There is no feeling of hatred or cribbing attitude toward the work they do. They earn money doing things they love to do and bring them joy - *and that love and joy beget love and joy.* They always express gratitude for what they have, give respect to others, value their time, and enjoy every moment. They don't have the idea of *wasting money* while giving it to others. This means that when they spend, they spend it with joy, happiness, and confidence. You could easily figure out that stress or fear is not a part of their lifestyle equation at all.

Happy and abundant people have the confidence to make enough when needed. They never worry when money goes away. That's why they are not stressed, anxious, or fearful about their future. They always have a positive attitude towards money. *They don't work for money; money starts working for them!*

Congratulations on reading this chapter! As you read this book, I believe you are enjoying your journey of attracting wealth and abundance. I am sure, after learning and implementing the concepts I have explained so far, you must be getting enough confidence to lead a happy and wealthy life. In this chapter, you'll learn why thinking and speaking positive words are necessary for us and how our feelings, thoughts, actions, and words can manifest in physical reality. Keep reading... Happy reading...

THE DOUBLE GAME

I feel many times that people show up their dual nature towards money.

The first kind of nature is pretending they aren't money minded and don't require money. They always **talk** negatively about money. They keep saying - *"Why have more money in life. We should not focus on earning more. It's not good to be money minded. I don't need more money as I've enough for my life. I'm happy with my earnings and am not greedy for more."*

And their second kind of nature keeps striking them; their inner conscience says - *"I need money. I don't have enough. I also need to live a luxurious life; I wish to have more money in my life."* This shows that they actually want to **manifest** something positive about money!

As you see, some people live with this dual nature and mentality toward money. On one side, they don't want to show that they desire money. They pretend they don't want to run behind money, so they keep saying that running behind money is not good, it's not good to be money-minded, and money is evil. While on the other side, they also want to have money to live a luxurious life. They also dream of money. They play the **double game** with money.

And that's when the real problem starts to happen in their lives. If you are also in the same category - **BE AWARE!**

I brought this topic to you because I want you to never play this double game. Never say or pretend what you don't want to get manifested. Because, ***what you say, can become a reality. You are energy; your words are also energy, and they have power. The moment you say something, you open a way for them to get manifested.*** If you say - I don't need money, the universe will say - ***Tathastu (so it is),*** and it may become a reality.

Ask your inner self - Do you really want to make it happen? Do you really want to manifest this? I'm sure your inner voice will say - **a big NO!**

So, if you don't want your words to become a reality, why are you creating and sending them to the universe in the first place itself? By saying negative words or having negative intentions for money, you are actually asking the universe to make your words true. Imagine, what if the universe listens to those words and fulfills your **non-intended wish**? Do you really want that to happen? No, right?

If your inner heart says that you like money and need it more for living a luxurious life, but at the same time you have the habit of expressing a negative attitude about money like - *I don't need money, I have enough, wanting more money is evil, money is bad, etc.,* **STOP THIS HABIT immediately!** Otherwise, you'll have to face the negative consequences in your life as many people are already facing directly or indirectly. Remember that - **Your words have power, and you attract what you say!**

THE POWER OF YOUR THOUGHTS, WORDS & FEELINGS

If you are unaware that human consciousness could affect the energy flowing in the universe or nature, this could be a piece of shocking information for you.

Masaru Emoto, *a Japanese businessman, author, and pseudo-scientist,* proved that human consciousness could affect the molecular structure of water. Since water is a natural resource covering more than 70% of the earth's surface, it directly or indirectly affects every being in its contact. Further, the human body has more than 70% of water, so any change in the molecular structure of water can dramatically impact our inner system. This includes all three systems - mental, physical, and emotional.

Emoto's experiment:

Dr. Emoto had done lots of research and experiments with water. His work shows that water molecules are affected by our environment, thoughts, words, and emotions. For over 20 years until he died in 2014, he studied the different water behavior when it is exposed to human words, thoughts, and feelings.

All his experiments are necessary for us to know because they help us understand how important it is to have positive thoughts and say positive words for money. It could be a disaster if we have negative thoughts or say negatively about money.

Dr. Emoto's extraordinary work on the water was first published in his **New York Times bestseller book *The Hidden Messages in Water***. He carried out exciting experiments with water at a critical point for freezing. He proved that words expressing emotions affect the crystals formed in the process. He claimed that words with positive emotions produce aesthetically pleasing physical molecular formations in the water, and those with negative emotions result in disconnected, disfigured, and "unpleasant" physical molecular formations. Emoto has also experimented with rice in water and claims that the words with positive energy induce a metabolic process known as fermentation, whereas those with negative energy make it rotten.

Dr. Emoto's conjecture evolved over the years, and his early work revolved around pseudo-scientific hypotheses that *water could react to positive thoughts and words and that polluted water could be cleaned through prayer and positive visualization.* He used **Magnetic Resonance Analysis** technology and **high-speed photographs** for his water studies.

After his profound studies and experiments, he said that - ***Water is the mirror that can show us what we cannot see. It is a "blueprint for***

our reality," and that emotional "energies" and "vibrations" could change its physical structure. All it takes is faith if you're open to it.

In his book ***The Hidden Messages in Water***, Dr. Emoto says - *"Water records information, and while circulating throughout the earth distributes information. This water sent from the universe is full of the information of life."*

The below picture shows a beautiful symmetrical shape rendered by the water crystals when exposed to the word **"Love & Gratitude"**:

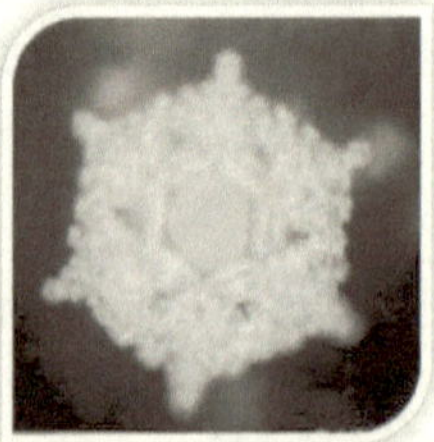

Love & Gratitude

As opposed to that, if we say **"You Fool"** and express our hate, the water crystals change to:

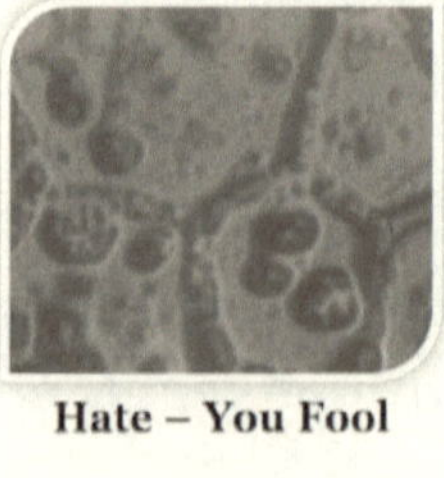

Hate – You Fool

See the following a few amazing water crystal photographs from Dr. Emoto's work:

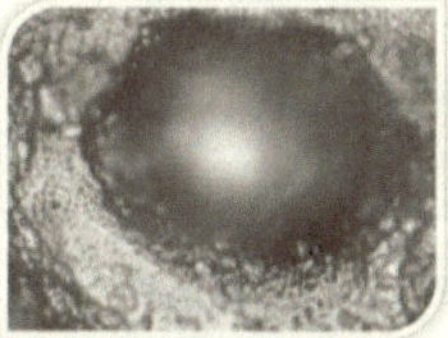

Evil

Thank You

Eternal

I Will Kill You

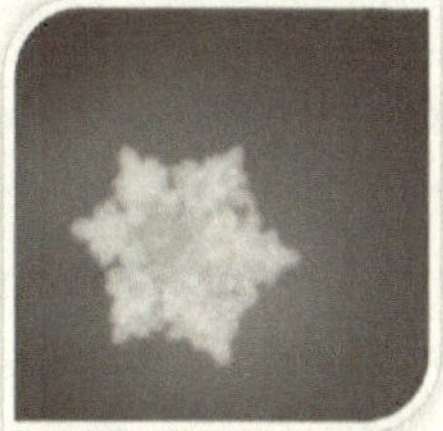

Goodbye

Friend

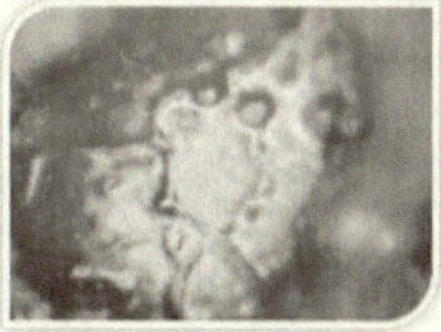

Before Buddhist Prayer
@ Fujiwara Dam

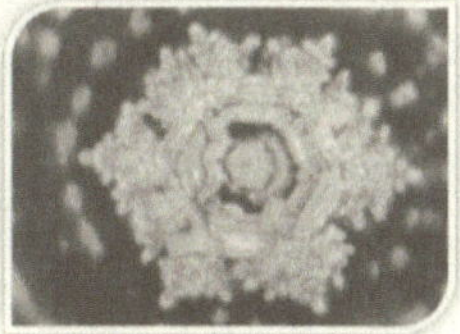

After Buddhist Prayer
@ Fujiwara Dam

Another famous experiment was **Lake Biwa**. The lake was heavily polluted and very dirty. Worse, the algae "kokanada" populated the lake, making it difficult to weed them out. It was the cause of the foul odors emanating from the lake.

In July 1999, 350 people prayed together in Lake Biwa. They prayed for the lake to be healed. By summer of that same year, the algae didn't come back. With clean-up efforts, the lake became clean again.

HOW IS IT RELATED TO WEALTH & ABUNDANCE?

Dr. Emoto's experiments showed that water can respond to human emotions, thoughts, words, and even written messages. These experiments are closely related to your wealth mindset. Since the water can understand the human intention and retain that energy, it signifies that your words, thoughts, and emotions can manifest in physical reality through the water changing its expression. You can make water more beneficial if you positively influence its structure.

As we know, we all are water beings with 70% water. Our thoughts & words can affect immensely the water inside us. If you keep saying negative things about money, you won't express the feeling of joy and happiness for money, and you keep saying that *you don't need money,* etc., then this negative energy will be exposed to your inner water system and will develop a negative environment there.

As you build this hostile environment inside, you also start attracting more negativity from outside. The law of attraction starts working, negativity starts attracting more negativity, and as a result, it becomes impossible for you to attract the wealth and abundance you actually want. If negative messages labeled on water jars can create such unpleasant frozen water crystals, imagine what being negative can do to your wealth and abundance.

This not only ruins your financial conditions but affects your health too. Exposing yourself to such an unhealthy hostile environment and thoughts adversely affects your health.

Conversely, if you are positive about your money, you express your true love and feelings about money, you respect money while talking about it, and you never say that *you don't need money*, etc., then your positive attitude towards money is exposed to your inner water system, and it develops a positive environment there for the money.

This positive environment starts attracting more positivity from outside, and as a result, you witness more wealth and abundance in your life. If you choose an attitude of love and appreciation, it will change you from within and energetically create a more sustainable and beautiful life for everyone else also.

Dr. Emoto's these experiments definitely raise our individual awareness to make a habit of "choosing better words before speaking," resulting in the natural attraction of wealth and abundance.

WEALTHY POINTS TO REMEMBER

❖ The mistake most of us make is - We hate our jobs, are not willing to do it with joy or a happy mood, always do it with a cribbing attitude, don't do it with honesty, and do it just for the paycheck. Avoid these mistakes if you want to live a life of abundance.

❖ Happy and abundant people have the confidence to make more when needed. *They don't work for money; money starts working for them!*

❖ What you say can become a reality. You are energy; your words are also energy, and they have power. The moment you say something, you open a way for them to get manifested. Your words have power, and you attract what you say!

❖ Dr. Emoto said - "Water is the mirror that can show us what we cannot see. It is a *blueprint for our reality*."

❖ Dr. Emoto's experiments proved that words, thoughts, and emotions can manifest in physical reality through the water changing its expression. These experiments hint to us to always use positive words for money no matter whether it is coming to us or away from us.

I'm grateful for your learnings from this chapter and wish you accept the money the way it is coming to you and thank it as it leaves you. Thank you, universe. Arigato!

9

Just Do It

I don't pay good wages because I have a lot of money; I have a lot of money because I pay good wages.

- Robert Bosch

The Pearl - *Break the chain of living in scarcity and start living in abundance.*

Have you ever been hurt by money in the past? Do you remember your parents telling you not to keep more expectations than they can fulfill? Have you ever gone through such a time when your parents asked you to compromise with your birthday gifts because they did not have enough to buy? Or have you gone through any such situation that made you believe that you or your parents didn't have enough money, so you must be careful before spending it? Take your time, recall your past and see what you get.

Many of us have been hurt by money in the past. We may not have received the exact birthday gifts we wanted; we may not have eaten in the luxurious restaurants we wanted or something similar. From a very young age, we observe that most of us have been programmed to have a few expectations regarding money. I remember a similar incident from my childhood - Once, my friend's father scolded him badly just because he had purchased a somewhat costlier birthday gift for his best friend. His father was even beating him for spending his hard-earned money just buying a gift for someone else. I still remember his father saying - *"You've no idea how hard I work to earn for the entire family; we could hardly get any money left over by the end of every month. We are struggling to save for our future, but you are just wasting money buying these gifts for your friend! You should understand the value of our hard work and money."*

In a family also, we often start blaming each other for spending (rather *wasting*) money, which sometimes leads to a serious argument. We start pointing fingers at each other for money. And it ends up with a hostile environment everywhere, making everyone unhappy, sad, irritated, and angry. **I feel sorry that *poor money* becomes the whole victim of this disharmony.**

In the above case, instead of berating my friend, his father could have encouraged and congratulated him for showing love, generosity, and openness in choosing the expensive gift. Don't you think there is a better way to teach a lesson to our children? Is scolding or beating the only option? Father's angry behavior was due to his own unhealthy relationship with money, which is now being transferred to his son. If the father had a good relationship with money, he would praise his son first and then teach him the appropriate amount to pay for the gifts.

When we go through several money situations throughout our lives, and if most of them are unhealthy, we start developing a sense that *"whatever we do, it won't be enough."* And this idea scares us even more. We start afraid of spending money on any "unnecessary thing." We fear that we are spending too much. We start doubting our own decision, e.g., after buying a comparatively costly dress, we regret and think we are cheated at that price. Even after getting a good deal, we feel we are wasting our money on unnecessary things. After paying for our holiday trip, we think we have spent more than the regular price, and if we had waited for more time, we could have gotten a better deal elsewhere. Also, we often enquire and search a hundred places even before buying the essential things.

We always regret money because we don't feel great about anything we purchase using it. We forget to enjoy the moment and the feelings money brings to us. We are only focused on the expenditure. We fail to live a life of true abundance. So, break this chain of *living in scarcity* if you want to get out of this cycle of worry, tension, anger, or fear. Experience abundance! ***Remember that the energy we spread into the universe is the energy that comes back to us.***

Congratulations on reading this chapter! This is the right time to experience the true wealth and abundance within. I would like you to experience something profound in this chapter. You will experience a strong connection with the universe. So, get ready for an exciting journey that will take you to another dimension of the universe where you will feel and attract true wealth and abundance.

A PRACTICAL WAY TO MANIFEST WEALTH & ABUNDANCE

I would love to now invite you for a beautiful abundance experience. I practice it regularly as it helps me a lot to get focus on my words, thoughts, and actions. As you now know, whatever you do, what you attract or are is directly related to what kind of thoughts you are creating inside. In other words, what frequency level you are vibrating at; what sort of frequency you are emitting and receiving. This practice is a powerful way to attract peace, wealth, and abundance in life.

Once again, welcome aboard! Be ready for a beautiful experience...

Close your eyes, and let's begin by taking three long deep breaths...

Breathe in wealth and abundance, and breathe out the feelings of uneasiness and unhelpful energy. Relax your body...

Breathe in again wealth and abundance; feel it as deep as you can, and now breathe out the old stagnant energy and unhelpful thoughts. Calm your mind...

One more time, breathe in wealth and abundance; experience the abundance going deep inside every cell of your body and spreading light everywhere. Finally, breathe out everything that no longer serves any purpose in your mind and body. Let go of your worries, tensions, troubles, and everything you are uncomfortable with. Relax your entire body... Experience the calmness inside and the quietness outside...

Now you are ready for a strong and profound connection with the universe - the source of infinite and powerful energy, the source of abundance.

Visualize the powerful, abundant energy of the universe - the source - in front of you. You are a small, tiny point of light connecting yourself to the source. Start feeling complete silence and peace around...

You are now silent, calm, and still. You are feeling the vibrations of wealth and abundance coming from the source. As you focus on the source, you see the supreme light - the bright shining divine star.

You are connected to the source, and your power is multiplied. You are now vibrating at the ultimate frequency of wealth and abundance. You are a receiver, vibrating at the same frequency as the giver - the source. You are now open to receiving this wealth and abundance into your mind, body, spirit, and everyday life. You are receiving the art and power to multiply this abundance in your daily life. You are opening yourself with complete trust and belief that this will continue to multiply in its energy and grow in its power. You are giving permission to yourself to completely surrender to it and accept the wealth and abundance you truly deserve.

Take one more long deep breath...

Now say - *I, myself* ***Ravi*** *(you take your name), allow myself to undergo this pure channel of wealth and abundance and receive the most I deserve from the source. I allow myself to become the master source of wealth and abundance now. I invite all universal powers, enlightened beings, and good energy to connect with me today and exchange the flow of wealth and abundance.*

I ask all universal energy that this *wealth and abundance practice* bring my highest deserving and highest reaching goals and potential. I accept that as I breathe in and open myself to this frequency, this positive energy will upgrade me from within and bring positive blessings to change my life for the longer term.

I ask for divine protection and guidance to manifest and attract all that I need to have and everything I have ever dreamed of. At the same time, I ask for cleansing of any negative energy inside that is not serving any purpose and doesn't sync with the high positive energy of wealth and abundance.

Permission is granted! The commission is granted for you to activate your higher frequency level. Permission is granted to receive this energy into your mind, body, and spirit. Permission is granted for you to own this new frequency of wealth and abundance. You are now allowed to accept this healing energy that will clear all your inner negative emotions and unhelpful energy about money. All your limiting beliefs about money are vanishing, and you are being blessed with empowering beliefs about money. All your traumas and darkness from the past are all gone now. All old negative energy is dissolving into dust, and you are activating your newer, higher, and positive energy.

The frequency of pure abundance is now turned on!

Experience a bright white light coming to the top of your head. Take another deep breath now...

Experience this light coming through your head, traveling through your chest, stomach, hips, base chakra, down your legs, and finally going out through your feet. Your body is now brightened and illuminated. Your mind, body, and spirit are activated and ignited with higher power and energy. Every cell in your body starts to vibrate and glow like billions of tiny bursts of sunshine. Every cell is growing, lighting, and vibrating with positive energy. These vibrations emit energy out of your body into your surroundings. Your body starts to glow from white to powerful warming orange like a sunset. This warm glow lifts your view higher into the sky, atmosphere, and space.

Look down and see this bright glowing powerful orange light emitting from you to the entire planet. ***You've become the master source of wealth and abundance now.*** You are showering the energy of wealth and abundance to all the beings on earth. The powerful energy of wealth and abundance has now become your integral part.

Take another deep breath and breathe in that energy you have created around you. Slowly breathe out and release all wealth and abundance into your surroundings.

Now slowly open your eyes and bring your consciousness back to your present moment. You are now a source of wealth & abundance, positivity & strength, hope & aspiration... Continue to remain in this feeling the whole day.

WEALTHY POINTS TO REMEMBER

❖ Meditation is a powerful way to program our subconscious minds. Meditation aims to wake up to the inner workings of our mental, emotional, and physical processes. It opens us to new possibilities and leads to creativity. Try once if you haven't practiced the wealth and abundance practice described in this chapter. This will take you to a space where you can receive positivity and welcome wealth and abundance. Remember, only when you welcome and encourage good things will they flow. So, let's give it a try!

I'm grateful for your learnings from this chapter and wish you experience the miracles of the universe as you connect with it. You become the channel of blessings for someone today. Thank you, universe. Arigato!

10

A Love Letter To Money

The rich invest their money and spend what is left; the poor spend their money and invest what is left.

- Jim Rohn

The Pearl - *Before attracting money, dare to lose it.*

Yes! This may sound weird to you, but this is true. Before attracting money, you should have the courage to lose money first.

When I read this for the first time in **Ken Honda's** bestselling book ***Happy Money***, it just blew my mind away. Ken Honda is a happiness expert and a bestselling author. He interviewed thousands of millionaires worldwide and studied with **Kodansha**, *one of the prestigious publishing houses in Japan,* called **How Ordinary People Became Millionaires**, which examined 10,000 millionaires and how they achieved success.

According to his study and analysis, he found one common thing in most of them - They all lost a lot of money and experienced failure and loss before accumulating wealth. They lost in various ways: through bad investments, employee theft, or failed businesses.

So don't get disappointed if you did not get success in your first attempt. Don't get discouraged by the first misfortune. Consider it as your learning phase and learn from your mistakes. You get one step closer to success when you learn from your mistakes. ***Believe in yourself, believe in the universe that after losing some, you will start attracting money - if, of course, you maintain a positive attitude and are open to receiving blessings from the universe.***

Finally, you reached here. Congratulations on reading this final chapter! This is not the ending; you will have a new beginning after this in your new world, ***your own world of wealth and abundance!***

Hope you learned many money lessons from previous chapters. I believe you learned ways to stop thinking about your money problems and understood how to upgrade your mindset with the power of Thank You. In this last chapter, I would appreciate it if you could bring down your feelings about money on paper. Remember, money is your best friend now. ***You will have to write a love letter to money!*** Believe me, this will be one of your most beautiful and unique experiences.

THE LOVE LETTER TECHNIQUE?

Do you know money is emotional? It needs your personal attention and time. It requires your acknowledgment of love and care. It's really a good idea to express your love to your best friend. What could be the best way other than writing a love letter to money! It's time to write a letter to money and express how your relationship developed over the years and how grateful you are for everything money does for you. Believe me, this will improve and strengthen your relationship with money.

You'll attract more money by writing a love letter to money. This works because you start to consider money as a person, a best friend in your life. When you consider money one of your life's most loving persons, you begin treating money the same way you treat other loved ones. You would show your respect, feel sorry when required, often express your gratitude, and take utmost care when it is coming to you or going far from you. In return, money loves coming to you and keeps coming with all its family members and friends.

Another reason the **love letter technique** works is its basic principle - ***what you appreciate appreciates and attracts more in your life!*** If you appreciate money in your life, money appreciates you!

By writing a love letter, you express how much you appreciate your money. This enhances your positive feelings and attitude toward money, eventually attracting more money in your life. Also, you know, whenever you don't appreciate someone, it moves away from you. The same becomes true for money.

I'm sure you would have written many letters to your beloved ones and don't require any format or guidelines for writing a letter, but still, if you need a sample, here you go.

I suggest you should write your letter covering all the below 3 aspects that exist in any relationship:

1) **Love aspect:** You can write how much you love your money, why you love money, how and when your love story started, etc. You can also write the number of qualities you like about money.

   For example, *"Dear money honey, thank you so much for always being in my life. Love you so much to the moon and back."*

2) **Role aspect:** You can write the essential roles money plays in your life, why those roles are vital for you, what all things money does for you, etc.

   For example, *"I love you, dear money. You always take care of me. Because of you, I am fulfilling all my needs; I can feed myself and quench my thirst. You have been fulfilling all my dreams since childhood. There was not a single day when you were not with me."*

3) **Gratitude aspect:** You can write why and how much grateful you are to have money in your life. Write why you want to thank money. Remember, gratitude is all about feelings. Connect your gratitude with feelings.

   For example, *"Thank you, money. I feel comfortable, secure, and satisfied in my life because of you. You are my energy booster. Because of you, I can sleep peacefully at night as I know I'm taken care of. I'm really thankful to you."*

A LOVE LETTER TO MONEY FROM *DR. NEELAM*

Below is what my wife, **Neelam**, wrote a beautiful letter to money **exclusively dedicated to this chapter.** ***(This is the original letter without any modification).***

A LOVE LETTER TO MY DEAREST MONEY - MY HONEY

Dear money honey, thank you so much for always being there in my life. Love you so much to the moon and back. Because of you, I'm living happily and comfortably. Thank you for loving me back, my darling. You are my lifeline; thanks for coming into my life happily and easily. I know you love me more than I do; you always love coming to me. I can buy anything with you. Thank you! I can wear my favorite clothes. Thank you for giving me this lovely home. Thank you for everything you do for me without any complaints. You always show as you care for me a lot. You never disappointed me; you always understand and support me.

Since childhood, you are always there with me. Because of you, I am fulfilling my needs; I feed myself and can drink water. You have been fulfilling all my dreams since childhood. There was not a single day when you were not with me. You are with me every moment, whether on my birthday or during school activities.

Dear money I want to say sorry to you as sometimes I doubt you will leave me. I'm sorry sometimes I feel guilty or sad about my spending, but now I understand that you will come back to me with your friends if you go with more love. I learned how you go and grow. I also understand that you travel and touch so many hearts. You are the channel of blessings for everyone.

Now, whenever I spend, I also spend with love and give blessings. I always remember that you will be a blessing to many people. Sorry for being possessive about you so far, but now I understand you better. I happily let you go and grow. Now I am not scared of losing you. Now I know that you have always loved me since childhood. There is no reason to doubt you.

Thank you for being with me all the time. I'm really grateful and blessed to have you. In fact, I feel really lucky to have you. I always got whatever I wanted. I have a comfortable life because of you. You are always with me in my bank account, wallet, and locker, enhancing me in all areas of my life.

Because of you, I'm able to help people who need you, which is great support from your side. You always come to me daily through many other routes, which is really commendable. I am truly in love with you. I m so grateful to you, big-big way.

I contribute to the different spiritual organizations only because you are in my life. I gift my friends and family all because of you. I can make them feel special. Thank you for making me feel special always. I am able to make someone's day special only because of you.

In every situation, you are there for me. I can forget myself but not you, my darling! You are the purest form of energy for me; I adore you. I can pay all my bills peacefully because of you. I feel so special that I can take care of my expenses peacefully.

I could travel to Maldives and USA because of you. I love traveling, and you fulfill all my traveling needs also. I am able to freely help my staff and house help because you are present in my life. I get so many blessings from them. A big thank you to my dear money, honey.

I'm sorry if I have hurt you sometimes. Sometimes I overspend you; I over-flaunt you. Please forgive me, thank you, I love you.

I really feel blessed, thankful, grateful, safe, and secure to have you. Thank you for finding me worthy of your love. Thank you so much.

Loads of love!!!

Your best friend, Neelam

EXERCISE TIME - *EXPRESS YOUR LOVE FOR YOUR MONEY*

I hope now you understand the magic of writing a love letter to money and are excited to write one. Aren't you? If yes, why make your best friend wait more! Grab your notebook and a nice big mug of coffee, and be ready!

Write a beautiful love letter to **YOUR** money. Remember that it's not about the fancy words you use in your letter; it's about your appreciation and the feelings you express about money. Don't be in a hurry; take your time. Try to cover all the aspects of relationships as told above.

After reading your love letter, money should have tears in its eyes! If money starts feeling that way, it will want to remain in your life forever.

I'm grateful for your learnings from this chapter. I hope you enjoyed writing a love letter to your own money. May the relationship between you and money flourish day by day. Amen! Thank you, universe. Arigato!

Conclusion

First of all, a big hug and congratulations to you. Most readers don't finish the book, but I believe you have read it entirely as you read this page. I hope you had a fantastic journey and learned the difference between your money and wealth goals. I'm sure you have a smile on your face as you read the final page of this book. You deserve a tap on your back!

You were introduced to your new friend, i.e., Money. You now have a clear understanding of wealth and abundance. Tips from all the chapters will help you create wealth in every part of your life. Now you have the keys to a life of success, fulfillment, wholeness, and plenty. Come forward, be open and receptive to all the good and abundance in the universe.

With the help of this book, you now know how to develop a sense of wealth & abundance in times of fear & insecurity. You now realize that money is not just a number or a piece of paper, but it is much more than that. You now understand the divine energy of money and learned the skills to attract wealth and abundance by practicing the power of Thank You.

I believe this book could serve its purpose of eliminating your limiting beliefs about money and enabling you to embrace the process of giving money, not just receiving it. It also made you realize that if you love and respect money, the money will be drawn towards you with the same love and affection. Now you can proudly say - **"I love you, money,"** and **"money loves me."**

I hope you will commit yourself and practice all the exercises described in this book one more time. This will strengthen your belief about money and re-program your subconscious mind to become open and receptive to all wealth and abundance the universe is to give you.

I'm sure you loved writing a love letter to your best friend, money. And I suggest you keep writing and acknowledging your feelings and emotions about money from time to time as it requires maintenance frequency.

I wish you great success in all your endeavors and a splendid life full of happiness and fulfillment.

Let me conclude with these powerful words from **Deepak Chopra,** *an Indian-American author, and alternative medicine advocate:*

In the process of letting go, you will lose many things from the past, but you will

find yourself. It will be a permanent Self, rooted in awareness and creativity. Once you have captured this, you have captured the world.

Arigato!

Ravi Lalit Tewari

REFERENCES

My knowledge and understanding of the importance of early morning hours have come from my personal experience, studying many books and websites. While it would be impossible to list them all here, I would like to specifically acknowledge the following books/websites which have proven particularly helpful to me in understanding the topic better:

Websites, blogs, and links-

[1] chopra.com
[2] financialgym.com
[3] goldenheartwisdom.com
[4] linkedin.com
[5] lornali.com
[6] masaru-emoto.net
[7] prosperitythinkers.com
[8] rise-indiaa.blogspot.com
[9] samatasoul.com
[10] thelawofattraction.com
[11] thewellnessenterprise.com
[12] www.betterup.com
[13] www.entrepreneur.com
[14] www.psychologicalscience.org
[15] www.researchgate.net
[16] www.speakingtree.in
[17] www.thecrimson.com
[18] www.verywellmind.com
[19] www.waterpeaceproject.org
[20] www.webmd.com
[21] Youtube videos
✓ https://www.youtube.com/watch?v=2bbHZusVgwo
✓ https://www.youtube.com/watch?v=3G94CdasEBI
✓ https://www.youtube.com/watch?v=tMQoD4sfEys

- ✓ https://www.youtube.com/watch?v=Jpm1Xumdn58
- ✓ https://www.youtube.com/watch?v=eo7eLYv4H_o
- ✓ https://www.youtube.com/watch?v=BLuPwPz-QIQ
- ✓ https://www.youtube.com/watch?v=g58z7hE6xiA
- ✓ https://www.youtube.com/watch?v=JFgwykD1EO4
- ✓ https://www.youtube.com/watch?v=OxOkR6EzSzw

DISCLAIMER

This book is for entertainment purposes only. Readers acknowledge that the author is not engaged in rendering legal, financial, medical, or professional advice. The content within this book has been derived from various sources. Please consult a licensed professional before attempting any techniques outlined in this book.

By reading this document, the reader agrees that under no circumstances is the author responsible for any direct or indirect losses incurred as a result of the use of the information contained within this document, including but not limited to errors, omissions, or inaccuracies. Adherence to all applicable laws and regulations, including international, federal, state, and local governing professional licensing, business practices, advertising, and all other jurisdiction, is the sole responsibility of the purchaser or reader. Neither the author nor the publisher assumes any responsibility or liability whatsoever on behalf of the purchaser or reader of these materials. Any perceived slight of any individual or organization is purely unintentional.

ABOUT THE AUTHOR

Software Developer, Author-preneur, Healer, Personal Counselor, and Law of Attraction Coach *Ravi Tewari* is the best-selling author of the book ***"from NIGHT-OWL to MORNING-LARK"*** and ***"SELF-MOTIVATION like CRAZY."***

He is the **founder & CEO** of an **IT company - IoT Meeting Hub™.**

Being a certified **Ho'oponopono, EFT, and Crystal healer,** he loves to conduct workshops and webinars to teach people about these ancient and profound techniques. His motivational classes & speeches are solely based on his own experiences and learnings that inspire many people to live a more rewarding and fulfilling life. He believes in sharing knowledge and giving 10x values.

He is also a **YouTube creator and vlogger** and loves to share various aspects of his life to motivate many others. He loves to keep this chanting every day - "May I be the channel of blessings of someone today!"

Other books Ravi has written:

manifest WEALTH & ABUNDANCE as you read

- ✓ from NIGHT-OWL to MORNING-LARK
- ✓ SELF-MOTIVATION like CRAZY
- ✓ GRATITUDE - LET THE UNIVERSE DO ITS MAGIC
- ✓ SEVEN STEPS TO SUCCESS
- ✓ KNOW AT A GLANCE

Contact him at ravinimbus@gmail.com

visit: https://www.amazon.com/author/neera

Join his community by CLICKING HERE

Explore more books by CLICKING HERE

MAY I ASK YOU FOR A SMALL FAVOR?

At the outset, I want to give you a big thanks for reading this book. You could have chosen any other book, but you took mine, and I appreciate this.

I hope you have at least a few actionable insights that will positively impact your daily life.

Can I ask for 30 seconds more of your time?

I'd love it if you could leave a review of the book. That will help me grow my readership by encouraging folks to take a chance on my books.

Keeping it straight - reviews are the lifeblood of any author.

It will take less than a minute of your time but will tremendously help me reach out to more people.

Please consider leaving an honest review on your favorite store if you enjoyed this book. And I'd love to see your review. Thanks for your support.

MAY I BE THE CHANNEL OF BLESSINGS FOR SOMEONE TODAY!

Preview of the book: YOUR THOUGHTS HAVE POWER

-- Start of Preview --

Why is it Essential to Know How to Utilize the Power of Thoughts & Make Them in Your Favor?

Our mind generates 60,000+ thoughts per day on average. Is this the exact number? Definitely, no? nobody knows the actual scenario, and do you think that all 60,000 thoughts that are released are equally powerful? No, they are not!

Consider a scenario where you have a rechargeable battery & you have connected three mobile phones to it for charging simultaneously. The battery has to contribute equally to all those three mobile phones at the same time. As a result, it will lose its potential quickly. Likewise, consider our mind like a powerful battery. However, if we distribute its potential in generating many thoughts simultaneously, they will soon drain the energy of our minds. As a result, no thought will be powerful, whether positive or negative. That's why it is an absolute need to understand how to utilize the power of thoughts & make them in our favor.

Now, consider the instance when the power of thoughts is not working in your favor. Instead, it is destroying and damaging us even more. I'm sure you would have noticed the related sad memories popping out of your mind when listening to some old sad songs. These tragic memories create a long chain of negative thoughts, and as a result, suddenly, we start feeling low at that time. In this case, you can see that the power of thoughts is working against you.

I hope now you would have a clear idea about how the power of our thoughts can make you happy or sad. Isn't it wonderful to know this secret?

How is the Power of Thoughts Aligned with the Power of the Universe?

We all are beautiful creations of this beautiful Universe. It is worth understanding that we all are energy, vibrating at a particular frequency. Science shows us that everything is made up of energy. It's the building block of all matter. The same energy that composes your body is also the one that makes every non-living being on this earth. Your motorbike, mobile, animals, plants, etc., are all composed of energy. It's all the same, constantly 'flowing' and changing form.'

The book you are reading, the object you are resting on, you & I are all energy. It means the Universe is an ocean of energy, and all vibrate at a specific frequency. It's impossible to isolate ourselves from the Universe because we are integral to it.

It simply proves that the thoughts you are creating are also energy. These thought energies connect with the particular energy frequency in the Universe. In other words, we can say that whatever thoughts (positive or negative) we create, they will connect with the same frequency present in the Universe.

When this connection happens, distance doesn't matter there. For example, when you read my book, my thought energy is connected with your energy irrespective of distance, time, space, and dimension. So, now our communication is happening at the thought energy level.

I hope your thoughts are now aligned and vibrating at the same frequency as the Universe's beautiful, powerful energy.

-- End of Preview --

GET YOUR COPY OF THE COMPLETE BOOK BY SCANNING THE BELOW QR CODE:

Other Books in *Self-Help Master Series*

Book 1: **SELF-MOTIVATION like CRAZY:** Increase Your Self-motivation, Learn About the Motivators & Practice 3 Magical Techniques Daily to Eliminate Negative Thoughts & Remain Self-motivated

Book 2: **from NIGHT-OWL to MORNING-LARK:** Learn to Wake up Early Like High Achievers to Own YOUR Morning & Practice the Not-So-Obvious Secrets to Elevate YOUR life

Book 3: **manifest WEALTH & ABUNDANCE as you read:** Stop Thinking About Your Money Problems, Upgrade Your Mindset with the Power of THANK YOU, & Embrace the Process of Giving the Money, Not Just Receiving It!

THANK YOU, READER, FOR SHOWING YOUR TRUST IN ME AND PURCHASING THIS BOOK.

JOIN MY COMMUNITY OR EXPLORE MY OTHER BEST-SELLING BOOKS: SCAN THE BELOW QR CODE

www.ingramcontent.com/pod-product-compliance
Lightning Source LLC
LaVergne TN
LVHW101613210926
848480LV00008B/391
9798215145128